STEFAN BOGNER // BEN WINTER

CARS & CURVES
A TRIBUTE TO 70 YEARS OF PORSCHE

DELIUS KLASING VERLAG

Der englische Begriff „Flow" steht schlicht für Fluss oder Strom. Und doch hat kaum ein anderer Begriff eine so vielseitige Verwendung gefunden. In der Medizin ist es der Luftdurchfluss einer Beatmung. In der Musik ist es die rhythmische Bewegung der Stimme zum Beat von Hip-Hop. Künstler im Allgemeinen scheinen diesem Begriff eine hohe Bedeutung zuzumessen, denn auch im Graffiti wird die Komposition zweier Werke als Flow bezeichnet. Am treffendsten erscheint aber vor allem die Betrachtung der Psychologie, die den Flow als einen Moment größten Glückes definiert, nämlich genau dann, wenn wir in einer Tätigkeit voll und ganz aufgehen.

Vielleicht ist aber auch die Summe dieser Interpretationen, die einen bereits auf der Silvretta Hochalpenstraße diese Glückseligkeit schon als Vorfreude empfinden lässt. Diese Vorfreude, wenn die Gedanken langsam erfassen, in Kürze Richtung Süden abzubiegen und den Sechszylinder im Rücken auf das Timmelsjoch zuzusteuern. Wenn die Atmung tiefer wird und der Luftdurchfluss sich erhöht. Genau wie die Hip-Hop-ähnlichen Beats des luftgekühlten Boxer-Meisterwerks, der nach Luft schreit, um in rhythmischen Bewegungen dem Gipfel entgegenzustürmen, während die Passstraße und die weißen Bergspitzen zu einem einzigen Kunstwerk zusammenfließen. Genau dann, wenn alle anderen Gedanken schwinden – durch die Suche nach der idealen Linie und dem besten Schaltpunkt. Genau hier, in dieser Haarnadelkurve und ihren unzähligen Abfolgen, genau hier ist der Flow zu finden.

The word "flow" seems so straightforward. Yet few other words have found such multifaceted and diverse application. In medicine, it refers to our breathing. In music, it's the rhythmic movement of the voice to a hip-hop beat. Artists in general appear to attribute a great deal of meaning to this word. Even in graffiti, the composition of two pieces of graffiti is referred to as flow. To me, however, the most fitting seems to be the view of psychology, which defines flow as a moment of great happiness, specifically when we are completely and utterly absorbed in an activity.

Perhaps it is also the sum of these interpretations that enables a feeling of bliss in the form of anticipation on the Silvretta High Alpine Road. This anticipation when the mind slowly grasps that the route will shortly turn southward and head up the Timmelsjoch with the six-cylinder growling from behind. When breathing deepens and the flow of air increases. Exactly like the hip-hop beats of the air-cooled boxer masterpiece screaming for air as it pounds its way towards the summit in rhythmic movements, while the road and the nature of the white mountain peaks flow together into a single work of art. Exactly when all other thoughts disappear – in the search for the ideal line and perfect shift point. Exactly here, in this hairpin bend and in the countless ones that follow – exactly here is where flow is found.

EDITORIAL

70 Jahre Porsche. Sieben Jahrzehnte einer außergewöhnlichen Erfolgsgeschichte. Sieben Jahrzehnte voller Innovation und ein mächtiges Fundament an Tradition. Wenn Menschen Geburtstag haben, schaut man nach vorn – bei Autos ist das genau anders herum. Die Ursache hierfür ist klar: Autos sind keine im Fluss befindlichen Individuen, sondern Ideen. Anders als wir sind sie statisch, vollkommene Kinder ihrer Zeit. Zu einem bestimmten Zeitpunkt verlassen sie die Entwicklungswerkstätten und Produktionshallen, werden dann eine technische Momentaufnahme, sind materialisierte Kreativität und Genie zum Anfassen.

Die Autos von Porsche ganz besonders: Zu jeder Zeit waren sie das ultimativ Machbare, Technologie an der äußersten Grenze des Vorstellbaren. Einerseits. Andererseits hatte man bei Porsche auch immer großen Mut zur Einfachheit. Durch beide Elemente gehören die Porsche jeder Epoche zum prägenden Lebensgefühl der jeweiligen Zeit, sie sind Kulturgut, manchmal auch Zeitgeist, auf jeden Fall aber immer bewegend. An einem Porsche kam und kommt man nicht vorbei – das wurde im Rennsport über mittlerweile 70 Jahre hinweg nachdrücklich bewiesen, ist an dieser Stelle aber einmal ganz anders gemeint. Substanziell. Emotional. Technologie-Faktisch. Vielleicht ist der große Porsche Beitrag zur Automobilgeschichte folgender: Wenn alle den einfachen und naheliegenden Weg gehen, findet Porsche die bis dahin nicht gedachte Abkürzung. Porsche ist logischer Nonkonformismus und kühler Pragmatismus zugleich. Porsche hat rebellische Autos für die Rebellen jeder Epoche gebaut, und das nicht aus hohlem Widerspruchsgeist, sondern aus einer tiefen Faszination an Klarheit und Endgültigkeit. Es geht und ging bei Porsche ja auch nie in erster Linie um eine Beschäftigung mit dem Außen, sondern um einen Wettbewerb mit

70 years of Porsche. Seven decades of an exceptional success story. Seven decades of innovation and an almighty heritage. When people celebrate a birthday, we usually look to the future. With cars. However, it works the other way around. The reason for this is obvious – cars are not individuals in a constant state of flux; they are ideas. In contrast to ourselves, there are static – absolute creations of their time. At a specific point in time, they leave the development workshops and production halls, which is when they become technical snapshots, creativity in material form and ingenuity you can touch.

Cars made by Porsche are very particular examples of this. Every time, they were the ultimate in feasibility; technology at the very outer limits of conceivability. Yet, at the same time, the people at Porsche always had the enormous courage of simplicity. Both of these elements have made the Porsches of every era a distinctive and intrinsic part of the essence of their time. They are cultural assets, sometimes part of the Zeitgeist and certainly always evocative. Nothing can beat a Porsche – something that has been clearly and definitively proven in racing over the last 70 years, although that is not the meaning in this particular case. The reference here is to substance, emotion, technology. Perhaps Porsche's great contribution to automotive history is the following: When all take the easy and convenient path, Porsche finds the as-yet undiscovered shortcut. Porsche is logical non-conformity and cool pragmatism in one. Porsche has built rebellious cars for the rebels of every era – not derived from a hollow spirit of protest and opposition, but from a deep fascination with clarity and conclusiveness. Porsche has never been primarily about a preoccupation with those around it, but about competing with itself. About being better, bolder, more definitive. Those who see themselves thus can hardly be accused

sich selbst. Besser werden. Kühner. Deutlicher. Wer ein solches Selbstverständnis hat, dem kann schlecht Kalkül unterstellt werden. Zur Porsche DNA gehören Strebsamkeit und Entschlossenheit der Ingenieure ebenso wie eine Kultur des Um-die-Ecke-Denkens, herrlicher Trotz und anrührendes Jetzt-erst-recht. Damit sollen die großartige Leistung und das Erbe anderer Automobil-Marken nicht geschmälert oder gar herabgewürdigt werden. Porsche ist aber etwas Besonderes. Und das wird durch den respektvollen Blick nach rechts und links nur noch besser sichtbar.

Beim Rückblick auf 70 Jahre Porsche kommt einem im ersten Moment nur eines in den Sinn: wie schnell das alles ging. Als sei es gestern gewesen. Vielleicht kommt uns der Porsche Werdegang auch nur deshalb so rasant vor, weil viele von uns einen Großteil der Entwicklung intensiv mitbekommen haben. James Dean in seinem kleinen, silbernen 550 Spyder könnte ein erstes Bild gewesen sein. Der trockene Sound eines luftgekühlten Boxermotors wirbelt in unseren Erinnerungen umher. Oder die Rennsport-Siege des legendären 956, Rallye Paris-Dakar mit dem 959 – Bilder in langsam verblassendem Kodachrome, aber immer noch lebendig, laut und intensiv. Erst gestern noch haben wir als Kind einem frühen 911 G-Modell hinterhergestaunt und jetzt plötzlich ist Porsche erwachsen geworden. Oder sind wir das? – Vielleicht haben Autos und Menschen ja doch mehr gemeinsam, als wir glauben: Wie sie werden wir in unserem Kern nicht alt, sondern reif. Wir verlieren im Lauf der Jahre nicht, sondern gewinnen an Substanz und Weisheit. Aus Geschichten wird Geschichte – hier sind wir mit unseren Autos ganz eng verbunden. 70 Jahre Porsche ist also eigentlich nicht nur ein Jubiläum der Sportwagenmarke aus Stuttgart-Zuffenhausen, sondern es ist unser Jubiläum. Man kann solche Autos nämlich nicht feiern, ohne auch an die Menschen zu denken. An die Denker und Macher, ganz besonders aber an die Porsche Fans. Sie haben jeden Porsche für einen Moment zu mehr als einer Idee werden lassen: Am Steuer, geparkt am Straßenrand, bejubelt an Rennstrecken, Gänsehaut vom Sound, elektrisiert vom Spiel des Lichts auf einer Karosserie. Aus Technik wird dann Emotion und Fluss.

Dieses Buch nähert sich den letzten 70 Jahren deshalb aus einer ganz besonderen Perspektive: Nicht die großen Momente werden hervorgehoben, sondern die vielen kleinen. Nicht die umfassenden Spannungsbögen sind es, die uns auf den folgenden Seiten antreiben, sondern ein paar Sekunden, Minuten, Stunden während einer Fahrt im Porsche. Auf den kleinsten Nenner gebracht sind es die Kurven, die eine Fahrt im Sportwagen so besonders machen, hier betritt die ewig junge Freude am Autofahren eine dritte Dimension. Zur Lust am Unterwegssein kommt das Fahren an sich, in den Kurven müssen Autos einen Offenbarungseid leisten. Plötzlich wird die Physik greifbar, die Art und Weise, wie sich ein Porsche bewegt, unterscheidet ihn von allen anderen Automobilen. Echte Fans behaupten, sie könnten selbst mit verbundenen Augen und Ohren feststellen, sobald sie in einem Porsche sitzen, allein an der Art, wie er Kurven absolviert. Mit Leichtigkeit und Präzision, einer ganz spezifischen Fahrzeugbalance, dem besonderen Feedback. Dies gilt für die

of cool calculation. Aspects of the Porsche DNA include the ambition and determination of its engineers as well as a culture of lateral thinking, exquisite defiance and a touching can-do attitude. This is in no way intended to belittle or even detract from the amazing achievements and heritage of other automotive brands. However, Porsche is something special. And this can only be made even more apparent by a respectful glance to the left and right.

Looking back on 70 years of Porsche, only one thing comes to mind in the first instance – how fast it all went. As if it were yesterday. Perhaps Porsche's evolution appears to have been so rapid purely because many of us have followed this development so intensely. James Dean in his little silver 550 Spyder may have been a first image. The dry sound of an air-cooled boxer engine whirling around in our memories. Or the racing victories of the legendary 956, the Paris-Dakar Rally with the 959 – images in gently fading Kodachrome, but nevertheless still vibrant, loud and intense. It was just yesterday that, as children, we gazed in wonder at an early 911 G-Model. And now, all of a sudden, Porsche has grown up. Or was that us? Perhaps cars and people have more in common than we believe. Just like them, our cores don't grow old, they just mature. We don't lose anything over the years; instead, we gain in substance and wisdom. Stories become history – this is what makes us very much like our cars. 70 years of Porsche is therefore really not just an anniversary for the sports car brand from Stuttgart-Zuffenhausen, but for us, too. You can't celebrate cars like this without also thinking of the people – of the thinkers and doers, but particularly of the Porsche fans. For a moment, they allowed every Porsche to become more than an idea – at the wheel, parked at the side of the road, cheered on at race tracks, goose bumps from the sound, electrified by the way the light dances on the body. This is when technology becomes emotion and flux.

It is for this reason that this book approaches the last 70 years from a very special perspective. It doesn't focus on the great moments, but on the many small ones. On the pages that follow, it isn't the all-encompassing arcs of achievement that drive us, but the few seconds, minutes or hours spent driving in a Porsche. Broken down to the lowest common denominator, it's the curves that make driving a sports car so special. This is where the eternally youthful joy of driving enters a third dimension. In itself, driving is all about the pleasure of being on the road. It's in the curves that cars have to declare their commitment. Suddenly, the physics become tangible. The way a Porsche moves differs from that of all other cars. True fans claim that even with their eyes and ears covered, they can tell if they're sitting in a Porsche purely from the way it corners – with lightness and precision, a very specific vehicle balance, distinctive feedback. The same goes for all Porsches, regardless of era and despite their substantial differences – somehow, somewhere that Porsche feeling is always there.

For us, it's about these moments of pure joy that arise in a Porsche and that always have a very specific setting – coordinates of longitude and latitude, road names and mile markers. CARS & CURVES is a homage to Porsche from the

Porsche jeder Epoche, auch wenn sie sich substanziell unterscheiden – irgendwie, irgendwo ist immer Porsche zu spüren. Für uns geht es also um diese Momente purer Freude, die in einem Porsche zutage treten und die immer einen konkreten Schauplatz haben. Breiten- und Längengrade, Straßennamen und Kilometerangaben. CARS & CURVES ist eine Hommage an Porsche aus der Perspektive des Fahrers: voller Emotion und versunken im Rhythmus der Straße. Für uns sind Kurven mathematische Gleichungen, absolut transzendent – andererseits erleben wir sie in vollkommen emotionalen Momenten. Früh am Morgen, wenn erste Sonnenstrahlen sanft über den Asphalt streichen, Gräser filigrane Schatten werfen. Mittags, abends und nachts im Scheinwerferlicht. Bei Regen und Schnee, Hitze und Staub. Duft von Macchia und Lavendel im offenen Seitenfenster, Sonnenstrahlen, die im Stakkato der Fahrt durch den Wald um uns blitzen, ein warmer Wind vom Meer, der es bis hoch in die Berge geschafft hat, auf der Haut. Kulturen und Kulinarik am Straßenrand. Der Moment, wenn nach einer langen Fahrt die Gang auf dem Parkplatz einer kleinen Pension einrollt, einer nach dem anderen, lachend, fluchend, schwitzend, durchgepustet, satt vom Leben, vom Speed, von den Kurven. Und dann: Abendessen. Für uns und unseren Porsche sind Straßen nicht einfach nur Bänder aus Asphalt oder Beton. Wir sehen ihre Schönheit und Logik, wir sehen, wie sie beginnen in ihrem Umfeld zu scheinen. Kurven, Strecken und Straßen machen ein flüchtiges Angebot. Vielleicht geht das ja nur uns so, aber wir finden, sie wirken, als könnten sie bereits im nächsten Moment verschwunden sein, als wären sie lediglich eine Chance.

Wer unser Projekt CURVES kennt, weiß: Auf unseren Fotos sind äußerst selten Autos zu sehen. Es geht uns darum, Platz für die Vorstellungskraft des Betrachters zu schaffen. CURVES ist demokratisch, die Straßen und Strecken gehören allen. Mit dem Buch „CARS & CURVES" wollten wir diesen formellen Ansatz aber konsequent aufbrechen und eine Auswahl der besten Porsche aus 70 Jahren auf mitreißenden Strecken inszenieren. Für uns war das vollkommen naheliegend: Seit wir denken können, sind wir im Porsche unterwegs, Porsche liegt uns im Blut, ein Porsche ist für uns das einzig logische Interface zur Straße. Deshalb ist CARS & CURVES kein kühles Konzept, sondern aus dem Fahren heraus entstanden – die in diesem Buch veröffentlichten Geschichten und Fotos gehören zum CURVES-Familienalbum. Sie sind entstanden, während CURVES entstand. Sie sind das Making-of hinter CURVES. Egal, ob es die Fahrt über einen zugefrorenen See ist, ob es sich um schnelle Runden auf Rennstrecken handelt, um alpine Bergpässe oder endlose Wüstengeraden – unsere fast meditative Perspektive bleibt. Aber wir materialisieren 70 Jahre Porsche. Den abgebildeten Autos geht es dabei wie den Straßen und Landschaften, die wir sonst einfangen: Sie werden nicht sachlich behandelt, sondern emotional. Sie werden zum Moment und zum Angebot. Vielleicht haben wir ja Glück und Sie tauchen ein. Nehmen Sie durch reine Vorstellungskraft Platz am Steuer, spüren kühlen Bergwind, hören den Motorsound, riechen den Duft von mürbem Leder, unverbranntem Benzin und heißem Öl. Spüren Sie aufgewirbelten Staub, Steine, Sand, Wasser und Schnee. Sonne auf der Haut oder Kälte in den Kleidern. Die Fotos in diesem

driver's perspective: filled with emotion and immersed in the rhythm of the road. For us, curves are mathematical equations, absolutely transcendent – yet we experience them in moments of sheer emotion. Early in the morning, when the first rays of sun wash gently over the asphalt, blades of grass casting delicate shadows. Midday, evening and by night chasing the beam of the headlights. In the rain and snow, heat and dust, the fragrance of macchia and lavender drifting through the open window, staccato rays of sunshine flashing around us as we drive through forests, our skin caressed by a warm wind that has made it all the way from the sea to the mountains. Cultural and culinary treasures at the side of the road. The moment, after a long drive, when the gang rolls into the car park in front of a small hotel – one after the other, laughing, cursing, sweating, windswept, full to the brim with life, with speed, with the curves. And then – dinner. For us and our Porsches, roads are not merely strips of asphalt or concrete. We see their beauty and their logic, we see how they begin to appear in their surroundings. The offer made by curves, tracks and roads is a fleeting one. Perhaps it's just us that think that way, but we find they look as though they could simply disappear at any moment, as if they are but a chance encounter. Anybody familiar with our CURVES project knows that cars rarely feature in our photos. It's about creating space for the viewer's imagination. CURVES is democratic, the roads and tracks belong to all. With CARS & CURVES, we wanted to make a conscious break from this approach and depict a selection of the best Porsches from 70 years on stunning stretches of road. For us, it was completely obvious – we've been traveling in Porsches for as long as we can remember. Porsche is in our veins; for us, a Porsche is the only logical interface with the road. That's why CARS & CURVES is not merely an abstract concept, but something created from driving. The stories and photos published in this book are part of the CURVES family album. They were created during the creation of CURVES. They are part of the "making-of" behind CURVES. Whether it's a drive across a frozen lake or fast laps on race tracks, trips along Alpine passes or endless desert straights, we stick to our almost meditative perspective. Yet we bring shape and substance to 70 years of Porsche. The cars in the images are like the roads and landscapes we normally capture – our treatment of them is not factual or objective, but emotional. They become part of the moment. Perhaps we're lucky and you're able to immerse yourself in them. Use the power of your imagination to put yourself at the wheel, feel the cool mountain breeze, hear the sound of the engine, breathe in the fragrance of brittle leather, unburnt petrol and hot oil. Sense the dust, stones, sand, water and snow kicked up in your wake. Feel the sun on your skin or the cold through your clothes. The photos in this book are not couch potatoes; every single one of them should be a mini action movie.

And then there are the stories. "Behind the scenes" becomes "centre stage". We wait eagerly for the Porsche 906 to be loaded into the freight plane on its way to the Laguna Seca race track in California – and just a moment later, we find ourselves on the Pacific Coast Highway. We attend as onlookers a meeting of 19 Porsche 918 Spyders on a journey through Switzerland and France. On the trip

Für uns geht es also um diese Momente purer Freude, die in einem Porsche zutage treten und die immer einen konkreten Schauplatz haben. Breiten- und Längengrade, Straßennamen und Kilometerangaben.

For us, it's about these moments of pure joy that arise in a Porsche and that always have a very specific setting – coordinates of longitude and latitude, road names and mile markers.

Buch sind keine Stubenhocker, jedes einzelne soll ein kleines Action-Movie sein. Und dann sind da noch die Geschichten. „Hinter den Kulissen" wird zu „Ganz vorn auf der Bühne". Gespannt warten wir mit dem Porsche 906 auf die Verladung ins Frachtflugzeug, auf dem Weg zur Rennstrecke Laguna Seca in Kalifornien, und finden uns einen Moment später auf dem Pacific Coast Highway. Als Zaungast wohnen wir einem Treffen von 19 Porsche 918 Spyder bei, die quer durch die Schweiz und Frankreich unterwegs sind. Bei der Reise im Cayenne entlang der deutschen und dänischen Küste bekommen wir den Sand nicht mehr aus den Schuhen, wenn wir im 911 Cabriolet durch Kalifornien räubern wird auf unserer inneren Jukebox dauernd eine Münze eingeworfen: Beach Boys, „Surfin' USA". Die plastischen Fotos eines Porsche 356 Carrera am Stilfser Joch lassen uns unwillkürlich ein imaginäres Gaspedal drücken, die Unterarme schwellen in jeder Kurve an. Porsche 956 auf der legendären Nordschleife des Nürburgrings – das ist Anlass für chronische Gänsehaut, gegensätzlicher als die verschlossen wirkenden Fotos des Typ 64 Berlin-Rom-Wagens und als gleich darauf die Reise im Macan durch Island geht es kaum. Und so weiter. Es ist ein absolutes Privileg, diese Autos fahren zu können, Autos, die man sonst in Museen und klimatisierten Garagen vermuten möchte. Der Punkt ist aber: Sie sind wirklich da draußen. Porsche werden gefahren, sie haben keine Angst, sich schmutzig zu machen.

Genau das ist auch der CURVES-Spirit, das „Soulful Driving". Diese Leidenschaft macht, dass wir Sie im Lauf der folgenden Seiten mit auf die Reise nehmen und ans Lenkrad der spannendsten Porsche aus 70 Jahren setzen wollten. „CARS & CURVES" ist unsere Art sich zu erinnern und zu feiern, ein Dankeschön an eine Marke, die wir lieben und die uns bewegt. Porsche. Unsere Welt. Unser Lebensgefühl.

in the Cayenne along the German and Danish coastlines, we simply can't get the sand out of our shoes. As we roam California in the 911 Cabriolet, we're constantly feeding coins into our inner jukeboxes: Beach Boys, Surfin' USA. The three-dimensional photos of a Porsche 356 Carrera on Italy's Stelvio Pass force us to step instinctively on an imaginary gas pedal, forearms bulging in every curve. A Porsche 956 on the legendary Nürburgring Nordschleife – that's a cause for some serious goose bumps. In stark contrast to one another are the enclosed-looking photos of the Type 64 Berlin-Rome car followed immediately by the trip through Iceland in the Macan. And so it continues. It's an absolute privilege to be able to drive these cars that you assume would otherwise live in museums and air-conditioned garages. But the point is that they really are out there. Porsches are being driven. They're not afraid to get themselves dirty.

And exactly that is also the CURVES spirit – "soulful driving". This passion makes us want to take you with us on this journey, through the pages of this book, and to put you behind the wheel of the most exciting Porsches of the last 70 years. CARS & CURVES is our way of remembering and celebrating them – a thank you to a brand that we love and that move us. Porsche. Our world. Our way of life.

Stefan Bogner ist Autor, Fotograf und Inhaber einer Designagentur – und ein leidenschaftlicher Porsche Fahrer. Mit seinen eindrücklichen Fotografien von Kurven, Kehren und Serpentinen hat er die Schönheit der Alpenpässe sichtbar gemacht. Sein Magazin CURVES und sein Bildband ESCAPES gelten unter sportlichen Automobilisten als perfekte Anleitungen zum Glücklichsein.

Stefan Bogner is a writer, photographer, founder of a Munich Design Agency – and a passionate Porsche driver. With his stunning photos of curves, hairpins and serpentines, he has captured the magnificence of the Alpine passes. Sporty drivers consider his magazine CURVES and his coffee-table book ESCAPES as the ultimate guides to happiness.

Ben Winter hat im Laufe der letzten 20 Jahre für die renommiertesten Tageszeitungen und Zeitschriften Deutschlands geschrieben, kann als früherer Motorrad-Rennfahrer die meisten europäischen und US-amerikanischen Rennstrecken am Geschmack der Kiesbetten erkennen, findet zu jeder großen Straße immer die viel schönere Umleitung und leidet an chronischem Fernweh. Als Sohn einer Ingenieurs- und Wanderprediger-Dynastie sieht der gelernte Fotograf und studierte Soziologe stets die Transzendenz aller Dinge.

Over the last 20 years, Ben Winter has written for Germany's most renowned newspapers and magazines. As a former motorcycle racer, he can recognise most European and American race tracks from the taste of their gravel traps. For every major road, he can always find the far more beautiful detour. And he suffers terribly from chronic wanderlust. As the offspring of a dynasty of engineers and itinerant preachers, the professional photographer and qualified sociologist always sees the transcendency of all things.

SCHWEIZ // SWITZERLAND
SUSTENPASS

PORSCHE 911 R
PORSCHE 911 R (2016)

PORSCHE 911 R

Starke Berge und starke Autos. Überschwängliche Momente im Anti-Gravitationsfeld des Sustenpass. Wenn die pure und unstillbare Lust an Kurven zum einzigen Daseinszweck wird, ist ein Porsche 911 R meistens nicht weit.

Intense mountains and intense cars. Exuberant moments in the antigravitational field of the Susten Pass. When the pure and insatiable lust for curves becomes the only raison d'être, a Porsche 911 R usually isn't far away.

Gleich um die Ecke vom Gotthardpass, zwischen Uri und Bern, zwischen Stier und Bär, liegt der Sustenpass. Schwerer, dunkler Stoff mitten im schroffen Herz der Schweizer Alpen. Ein Pass mit überschwänglicher Schönheit und hypnotischem Rhythmus. Man muss den Susten nicht fahren, wenn es um große, europäische Fluchten geht, da sind die West-Ost-Talstrecken in Alpenquerrichtung oder die ausgetretenen Nord-Süd-Trassen am Gotthard oder San Bernardino deutlich effizienter. Aber der Susten hat eine Leidenschaft für den Moment. Und wenn man diese Fahrt im alten und neuen Porsche 911 R unternimmt, öffnet sich unweigerlich eine Tür in die Vergangenheit.

Die R-Modelle waren noch nie Porsches interkontinentale Direktverbindung oder mächtige Blockbuster. Stattdessen sind sie die winklige Nebenstraße ins Herz der Marke. Wenn diese glorreichen Geräte ohne Umschweife mit allen Konventionen brechen und ungeniert zur Sache kommen, ist das pures Glück. Willkommen in einem Winkel der Marke Porsche, in dem die pure Lust der Ingenieure am Extrem zur Doktrin wird. Alles beginnt mit dem ersten 911 R, den ein junger Ferdinand Piëch zum Über-Neunelf macht, zum leichtesten Porsche 911 aller Zeiten. Am Susten materialisiert sich das auch noch 50 Jahre später zu einem rohen, ungefilterten Vergnügen: Motorsound, bei dem sich wohlig alle Haare aufstellen, Einlenken wie mit einem Liter Espresso im Blut, aus jeder Kurve und Drehzahl heraus ein markiger Antritt der ganz transzendenten Sorte. Dass der Porsche 911 R von 2016 das etwas anders angeht, liegt auf der Hand. Der 911 ist heute kein Teenager mehr, er ist reifer, weiser und erwachsener als damals. Aber wenn im modernen 911 R 500 handgeschaltete PS auf 1370 fahrfertige Kilogramm treffen, ist auf einmal wieder alles ganz verschwitzt und wild und atemlos. Die pure Lebenslust hetzt da im Duett den Berg hinauf. Jetzt-erst-recht-Attitüde beim feierlich zelebrierten Zwischengasgeben. Man muss es ganz klar sagen: Das sind Autos zum schönen Schnellfahren.

Right around the corner from the Gotthard Pass, between Uri and Bern, between bull and bear, is the Susten Pass. Heavy, dark stuff in the jagged heart of the Swiss Alps. A pass of exuberant beauty and hypnotic rhythm. If it's a great European escape you're looking for, you really shouldn't drive the Susten – the west-east valley roads across the Alps or the well-worn north-south trails at the Gotthard or San Bernardino are considerably more efficient. But the Susten has a certain passion for the moment. And if you drive this road in an old and a new Porsche 911 R, it inevitably opens a door to the past.

The R models were never Porsche's direct intercontinental routes or huge blockbusters. Instead, they are the small, winding side roads into the heart of the brand. It's nothing less than sheer joy when these glorious machines break all conventions without digression, and get unabashedly to the point. Welcome to a corner of the Porsche brand where the lust for pure engineering in its extreme become doctrine. It all starts with the first 911 R that a young Ferdinand Piëch turned into the Über-911, the lightest Porsche 911 ever. Even 50 years later, it still materialises itself on the Susten Pass as raw, unfiltered joy – an engine sound that makes all your hairs stand on end, turning in like you have a litre of espresso pumping through your veins, an almighty kick of the totally transcendent kind out of every bend and rev. It's pretty obvious that the 2016 Porsche 911 R is a somewhat different proposition.

The 911 of today is not a teenager anymore – it's wiser, more mature and more grown up than it was back then. But when 500 manually shifted hp meet 1370 road-ready kilograms in the modern 911 R, everything suddenly gets sweaty, wild and breathless all over again. The sheer lust for life dashes up the mountainside in tandem. A now-more-than-ever attitude paired with enthusiastic double de-clutching. Say it loud and clear – these are cars that simply love to be driven fast.

18 — PORSCHE 911R — 911R (2016) / SUSTENPASS / SCHWEIZ — SWITZERLAND

SCHWEIZ // SWITZERLAND
GRIMSELPASS

PORSCHE 356 SPEEDSTER

PORSCHE 356 SPEEDSTER

Cool und soulful am Grimselpass – wenn sich der legendäre Porsche 356 Speedster an dieser klassischen Serpentinenstraße der Schweiz einnistet, wird Intensität größer geschrieben als operettenhaftes Drama.

Cool and soulful on the Grimsel Pass. When the legendary Porsche 356 Speedster gets in about this classic Swiss serpentine, it delivers intensity of operatic proportions.

Am Totensee, in Sichtweite des Schreckhorns, macht der Grimselpass dem nicht weit entfernten Gotthardpass Konkurrenz – die Strecke ist aber bei weitem nicht so martialisch wie man es angesichts dieser Koordinaten vermuten könnte. Moderate Steigungen zwischen einer Vielzahl von Serpentinenkehren in dramatisch hochalpinem Panorama machen „die Grimsel" aus, das spricht für tiefen Genuss einer Fahrt und weniger für sich hetzende Effektmomente. Für die mentale Mund-zu-Mund-Beatmung des inneren Fahrspaß-Rebellen beim Kurvensurfen taugt ein hochemotionaler Porsche 356 geradezu ideal, und wenn es dann noch die intensive Speedster-Version von 1954 ist, wird aus den etwas über 30 Kilometern zwischen Innertkirchen und Gletsch eine Feierstunde.

Als Reaktion auf US-Kundenwünsche konzipierte Porsche Mitte der 1950er-Jahre dieses kleine und leichte Gerät mit seiner kurzen Windschutzscheibe, den seitlichen Steckscheiben und sportlichen Schalensitzen. Wichtiger ist allerdings nicht, was der kleine Sportwagen hat, sondern was nicht: eine Heizung zum Beispiel. Oder irgendwelche Ablagen. Der mit Sicherheit berühmteste Besitzer, der tragisch verunglückte James Dean, dürfte auch idealer Fahrer gewesen sein: Sonnenbrille statt Sonnenblende. Anti-Establishment. Der Speedster wollte die rebellische und reduzierte Version des 356 sein, schockierend ehrlich und geradezu existenziell reduziert. Seine drahtige Bauweise, das geringe Gewicht und kompakte Abmessungen machen ihn auf kurvigen Strecken zum exakt positionierbaren Wunder an Fahrfreude. Natürlich kann ein Speedster auf abgesperrten Strecken auch gewaltig aufdrehen, am Grimselpass muss das aber nicht sein. Während über einem die Bergdohlen kreisen, lässt man sich jetzt lieber vom Fahrtwind durchpusten, freut sich am Rhythmus der Strecke und dem ehrlichen Charakter des Porsche 356 Speedster. Saftig ausgedrehte Gänge, kerniger Motorsound, zupackender Vorwärtsdrang. Sägen am Lenkrad, Fahren mit Schwung, Stil und Köpfchen. Pure Freiheit, nicht weniger.

At the Totesee, within sight of the Schreckhorn, the Grimsel Pass presents stiff competition to the nearby Gotthard Pass. However, the road is not nearly as menacing as its coordinates would have you believe. The Grimsel is defined by moderate inclines dispersed among a plethora of serpentine hairpins set against a dramatic Alpine panorama. The result is a drive that is more deeply pleasurable than frantically action packed. A highly emotional Porsche 356 is utterly perfect for the mental mouth-to-mouth resuscitation of your inner boy racer as you surf the bends. And when it's the 1954 Speedster version, the roughly 30 kilometres between Innertkirchen and Gletsch are an absolute joy.

Reacting to the wishes of its American customer base, Porsche conceived the small, lightweight machine with its short windscreen, removable side curtains and sporty bucket seats in the mid-1950s. More important than what the diminutive sports car has, however, is what it doesn't have – like heating, for instance. Or any storage cubbies whatsoever. Surely its most famous owner, the tragically lamented James Dean, could also be considered its most ideal driver – sunglasses replace sun visor. Anti-establishment. The Speedster wanted to be the rebellious and minimalist version of the 356 – shocking in its honesty and positively existential in its bare essentials. Its wiry construction, low weight and compact dimensions make it a perfectly positionable joy to drive on winding roads.

You can obviously push a Speedster really hard on a closed road, but you don't have to do that on the Grimsel Pass. With the ravens circling above you, it's better simply to let yourself go with the flow, enjoy the rhythm of the road and the honest character of the Porsche 356 Speedster. Lusciously high revs, throaty engine sound, emphatic energy. Working the wheel, driving with vigour, style and wits. Pure freedom – nothing less.

36 – PORSCHE 356 SPEEDSTER / GRIMSELPASS / SCHWEIZ – SWITZERLAND

CARS & CURVES

FRANKREICH // FRANCE
SEEALPEN
MARITIME ALPS

PORSCHE 911 GT3
TOURING-PAKET
PORSCHE 911
CARRERA T

911 GT3 TOURING-PAKET
911 CARRERA T

Sorry, Finnland, Schweden, Korsika, Griechenland und all ihr anderen, aber wenn jemand „Rallye" sagt, denken alle „Monte Carlo". Tage der langen Messer im Porsche 911 GT3 Touring-Paket und 911 Carrera T. Passt.

Sorry Finland, Sweden, Corsica, Greece and all the others, but when someone says 'rally', we all think 'Monte Carlo'. Days of the long knives in a Porsche 911 GT3 Touring Package and 911 Carrera T. Perfect.

Porsche hat die Rallye Monte Carlo gewonnen, zwischen 1968 und 1970 gleich dreimal in Folge, 1978 noch einmal, nicht zu vergessen der frühere GT-Klassensieg 1965 – und immer waren das alles kleine Sensationen, selbst für einen Motorsport-Routinier wie Porsche. Die Monte legt sich einem nicht schnurrend vor die Füße, auch wenn man das beim Anblick der zivilisierten Fotos vom Zieleinlauf in Monaco noch vermuten könnte. In Wirklichkeit aber tut das Monster in den Seealpen alles, um Fahrer bis ins Mark zu erschüttern und Autos zu blamieren. Hinter den Corniches, den Panoramastraßen an der Cote d'Azur, beginnt eine wilde Welt mit schmalen Straßen durch eine schroffe Landschaft. Die Serpentinen-Kilometer hoch zum legendären Col de Turini sind da nur ein heftiger Einstieg. Danach wird es erst so richtig hart. Vor allem aber: wunderschön.

Die Rallye Monte Carlo lässt sich freilich nicht nachfahren, da müsste man sich schon selbst den feuerfesten Dress überziehen und im Renntempo Gas geben. Was aber geht, ist eine Tour durch die Magie der Landschaft, in der alles passiert. Die zuziehenden Kurven, die frostzerbeulten Straßen, der Wechsel zwischen mediterraner Milde und alpinem Frost. Die Wintersonne. Am besten in einem Porsche, der kompromisslos schnell und aufgeschlossen zugleich ist. Der Leichtigkeit mit Autorität verbindet. Und deshalb machen wir uns mit einem 911 GT3 Touring-Paket auf die Reise, im Windschatten folgt der 911 Carrera T. Die beiden gehen gerade so viel Kompromiss ein, dass es zur tückischen Strecke und den vielen Kilometern passt, schalten dann aber gefühlt auf Angriffsmodus. Die wollen nur spielen, oder etwa nicht? Läuft insgeheim die Stoppuhr? Bitterböse Beschleunigung, flammendes Handling, extrovertierte Charaktere. Der GT3 Touring-Paket ist die reine Lehre und regelrecht präzisionsvernarrt, ein hypnotischer Charakter, der Carrera T hat immer einen etwas weiteren Blickwinkel. Sektionszeit versus Emotion. Auf diesen Strecken funktioniert beides. Und am Ende meint man dann tatsächlich den Geist der Rallye inhaliert zu haben.

Porsche won the Rallye Monte Carlo three times in a row between 1968 and 1970, again in 1978 and let us not forget the earlier GT class victory of 1965 – and all of them were minor sensations, even for a motorsport veteran like Porsche. The Monte is not something that simply falls purring at your feet – despite what looking at the civilized photos from the finish line in Monaco may lead you to believe. In reality, the monster in the Maritime Alps does absolutely all it can to disgrace cars and shake drivers to their core. Beyond the corniches, the panoramic roads along the Cote d'Azur, begins a wild world of narrow roads through a rugged landscape. The intense miles of serpentine leading up to the legendary Col de Turini are just the start of it. After that, it gets really tough. But, above all, absolutely stunning.

The Rallye Monte Carlo is not easy to replicate. You would have to get all kitted out in the appropriate fire-resistant gear and attack the course at race speeds. What you can do, though, is take a trip through the magical landscape in which it all takes place. The tightening curves, the ice-damaged roads, the switch from mild Mediterranean air to Alpine frost. The winter sunshine. The best way to do this is in a Porsche that is both uncompromisingly fast and outgoing; that pairs lightness of touch with authority. And that's why we're doing it in a 911 GT3 Touring Package, with a 911 Carrera T following in our slipstream. The two accept just the right amount of compromise for the treacherous route and high mileage, yet feel like they then switch into attack mode. Just wanna play, do you? Stopwatch running secretly somewhere? Venomous acceleration, scorching handling, extroverted character. The GT3 Touring Package is the real deal and utterly infatuated with precision. A hypnotic character, the Carrera T always has a somewhat broader perspective. This is stage time versus emotion – both work very well on these roads. And by the end of it, you truly feel like you've inhaled the spirit of the rally.

ISLAND
ICELAND

PORSCHE
PANAMERA TURBO S
E-HYBRID
SPORT TURISMO

PORSCHE PANAMERA TURBO S E-HYBRID SPORT TURISMO

Endlich darf er raus. Porsche Panamera Turbo S E-Hybrid Sport Turismo am Flughafen Reykjavík. Runter aufs Rollfeld. Touchdown. So beginnt eine mysteriöse Reise mit geheimnisvoller High-Tech-Troll-Energie.

It's finally released. The Porsche Panamera Turbo S E-Hybrid Sport Turismo at Reykjavík Airport. Touchdown. It marks the start of a mysterious journey with secretive high-tech troll energy.

Irgendwann steht der 680-PS-Panamera am Tor des Flughafens und die Schranke hebt sich langsam. Elektro-Modus. Herzhaft Gas geben und die 100 Kilowatt-Elektromaschine mit ihrem deftigen Drehmoment schlenzt den Porsche beinahe geräuschlos ins Freie. Der Turbo S E-Hybrid fühlt sich an wie Island: an der Oberfläche ruhig und souverän, aber darunter versteckt sich gewaltige Energie. 100 Prozent der Energie Islands stammt aus natürlichen Ressourcen, vulkanische Superkräfte halten die wilde Insel des Nordmeers an der Erdoberfläche. Der Porsche scheint diese Wesensverwandtschaft sofort zu spüren, er pfeilt zum Stadtrand und zielt dann in die Wildnis hinaus.

Offene Straßen, zerprügelt von eiskalten, rabenschwarzen Wintern und dem Tauwetter eines kurzen Sommers. Geysire kochen, heiße Quellen dampfen, Moos und Flechten krallen sich mit trotziger Entschlossenheit auf vulkanische Felsen und am Strand lassen sich durchsichtig-blaue Eisschollen von der Brandung auf schwarzen Lava-Sand tragen. Wasserfälle stürzen sich in ihre Klamm, Regenwolken ertränken das Land in einer Fünf-Minuten-Sintflut und dann explodiert ein Regenbogen über den Eisgipfeln der Berge am Horizont. Im Panamera fahren heißt jetzt: überirdische Traktion, völlige Ausgeglichenheit. Wenn dann aber die ersten Kurven in den Lava-Hängen auftauchen, wirft er sich mit entschlossener Leidenschaft in die Kehren. Wird zur Kurve. Fahren ohne Filter. Auf einer langen, einsamen Geraden am Ende der Welt testen wir die Launch Control. Und das hat beängstigende, atemberaubende Züge. Vulkanisch eben. Elektroantrieb und Biturbo-V8 verschmelzen im Panamera Turbo S E-Hybrid zu einer homogenen Einheit, aus dem brutalen Anfahrdrehmoment der E-Maschine wächst der knochentrockene Punch der Turbolader und wird dann von der zuschnappenden Drehzahlgier des Achtzylinders komplimentiert. Wann was aufhört oder anfängt, ist nicht auszumachen. Dies ist eine Maschine, die dem Wort „Systemleistung" eine ganz neue, poetische Komponente verleiht. Muss Isländisch sein.

At some point, the 680 hp Panamera is standing at the airport gates and the barrier slowly lifts. Electric mode, foot down and the Porsche's substantial torque sends it hurtling almost noiselessly into the open. The Turbo S E-Hybrid feels like Iceland – calm and refined on the surface, but with colossal reserves of energy hidden beneath. 100 percent of Iceland's energy comes from natural resources, volcanic superpowers keeping the wild island in the North Sea rooted to the Earth's surface. The Porsche seems immediately to sense this affinity and heads straight out of town and into the wilderness beyond.

Opens roads, battered by ice-cold, pitch-black winters and the thaw of a brief summer. Geysers boil and bubble, hot springs spout steam, moss and lichen crawl up the volcanic rocks with defiant determination, while the surf forces translucent blue ice floes onto the black sand of the lava beaches. Waterfalls tumble into the ravine; rain clouds drench the land in a five-minute deluge and then a rainbow explodes over the icy peaks on the horizon. Driving a Panamera here means unearthly traction, utter equilibrium. However, when the first curves appear in the lava slopes, it throws itself into the bends with passionate determination – becomes the bend. This is driving without a filter. On a long, lonely straight at the ends of the Earth, we test the Launch Control, and it has fearsome, breathtaking pull – volcanic, even. The electric drive and biturbo V8 in the Panamera Turbo S E-Hybrid fuse to become a single, homogenous unit. The bone-dry punch of the turbocharger emerges from the brutal starting torque of the electric motor and is then complemented by the biting, high-revving voracity of the eight-cylinder. You simply can't tell where one ends and the other begins. This is a machine that gives a whole, new, poetic component to the term "system power". It must be Icelandic.

DEUTSCHLAND // GERMANY
USA – KALIFORNIEN // CALIFORNIA
PORSCHE REUNION, MONTEREY

PORSCHE 906

PORSCHE 906

Rennwagen mit Straßenzulassung klingt gut. Aber kann man eigentlich in einem Porsche 906 zur Porsche Rennsport Reunion nach Laguna Seca/Kalifornien fahren? Aus eigener Kraft, auf eigener Achse? – Klar, kann man!

A road-legal race car sounds all very well. But can you really drive a Porsche 906 to Laguna Seca, California for the Porsche Rennsport Reunion? Under your own steam? Of course you can!

Morgens aufstehen, die Glasfaser-Flügeltür des Porsche Carrera 6 (wie der 906 eigentlich heißt) öffnen, dann einsteigen. Der Wagen ist kompetent gewartet und ganz gut in Schuss, was so viel heißt wie: Er springt nach nur wenigen Umdrehungen des Anlassers an. Klingt tief, kernig, sauber. Trotz Rennkupplung gelingt Anfahren ohne Abwürgen, raus aus der Werkstatt des Porsche Museum, rauf auf die Straße. Beim Bäcker staunen die ganz schön, als der 906 ausrollt, aber hier in Stuttgart ist man in Sachen Porsche so einiges gewohnt. Alle schauen, ein paar freundliche Kopfnicker gibt es ebenfalls zum Kaffee und zur Brezel, mehr wäre für Schwaben ja auch schon fast aufdringlich. Und dann eben die Autobahn. Im Porsche 906 ist das nicht unbedingt Idealbetrieb, der Rennwagen mag die wechselnden Drehzahlen auf Rundkursen und bei Bergrennen deutlich lieber als gleichbleibende Autobahn-Richtgeschwindigkeit. Also bekommt er Drehzahlwechsel. Mal Schlendern im großen Gang, dann wieder eine kleine, frivole Speed-Einlage. Nichts Wüstes natürlich. Nur eben ein wenig Spaß haben. Der Fahrer trägt Gehörschutz, das ist ein paar Zentimeter von einem Zweiliter-Sechszylinder-Boxermotor entfernt ganz angenehm. In Frankfurt geht der Carrera 6 ins Flugzeug, brav wartet der Porsche auf Paletten verzurrt im Regen auf seine Verladung. Dann darf der Renner 5780 Meilen lang im Frachtraum von der Targa Florio und Le Mans träumen. Bis er es in Los Angeles aus dem Zoll geschafft hat, ist es spät in der Nacht. Einen hartgesottenen Langstrecken-Rennwagen stört das nicht, er wirft die Scheinwerfer an und stürmt raus auf die Highways. Nur noch wenige Stunden bis zur Startaufstellung oben in Monterey. Am Morgen ist er dann unterwegs auf dem Pacific Coast Highway in Richtung Norden. Kurven, Kurven, Kurven. Irgendwie hat der Sechszylinder bereits den sonnigen California-Groove. Und dann fährt er rein in die ockerfarbenen Hügel der Laguna Seca. Das Publikum sieht das deutsche Kennzeichen, die Fliegen an der Windschutzscheibe und nickt anerkennend. Porsche Rennsport Reunion.

Get up in the morning, open the glass-fibre gullwing doors of the Porsche Carrera 6 (as the 906 is actually called) then climb in. The car has been competently maintained and is in very good shape, which roughly translates into: it fires up after just a few turns of the starter motor. The sound is deep, throaty, clean. Despite the racing clutch, it's possible to pull away without stalling – out of the workshop at the Porsche Museum and onto the road. There's no shortage of stares at the baker, but the folks here in Stuttgart are used to all sorts of things when it comes to Porsche. Everybody looks and there are a few friendly nods of the head to go with my morning coffee and pretzel. For Swabians, any more than that would be almost intrusive. And then comes the autobahn. This is not necessarily ideal territory for the Porsche 906. The race car likes the varied revving of circuits and hill climbs far more than constant autobahn speeds. So, it gets some varied revving. We saunter along in high gear for a while, then switch to a low, frivolous ratio. Nothing too disorderly, you understand, just a little bit of fun. The driver is wearing ear protection, which makes life a couple of centimetres from a two-litre six-cylinder boxer engine very pleasant. The Carrera 6 is loaded onto a plane in Frankfurt – the Porsche strapped to palettes and awaiting its turn patiently in the rain. Then the race car can spend 5780 miles in the cargo hold dreaming of the Targa Florio and Le Mans. It's late into the night before it clears customs in Los Angeles. This doesn't bother a hardened endurance racer one bit. It throws on its headlamps and storms out onto the highways. Just a few more hours to go before the starting line-up in Monterey. The next morning, it's on the road heading north on the Pacific Coast Highway. Curves, curves, curves. Somehow, the six-cylinder is already in the sunny Californian groove. And it drives into the ochre hills of Laguna Seca. The spectators see the German number plate, the flies on the windscreen and nod appreciatively. Porsche Rennsport Reunion.

CARS & CURVES   PORSCHE REUNION / DEUTSCHLAND – GERMANY – USA / PORSCHE 906 – 87

SCHOTTLAND // SCOTLAND
NORTH 500

PORSCHE
PANAMERA 4
E-HYBRID

PORSCHE PANAMERA 4 E-HYBRID

Pflicht für Straßensammler: die North Coast 500 rund um Schottland. 500 atemberaubende Meilen entlang der Küste, quer durch die Highlands. Der Porsche Panamera ist für diese Reise vollendet souverän.

An absolute must for road collectors – the North Coast 500 around Scotland. 500 breathtaking miles along the coast and through the Highlands. The Porsche Panamera is utterly perfect for this trip.

In Glasgow geht es los, die graue Stadt am River Clyde wird aus dem Süden ankommend zum westlichen Tor der schottischen Highlands. Im Loch Lomond National Park zeigen die Highlands gleich zum ersten Mal die Zähne, das Land ist urwüchsig, herb und düster. Und dann fährt man sich sowieso schwindelig, in einen Rausch von großartiger Natur, majestätischer Landschaften und Kurven, Kurven, Kurven. Über Bridge of Orchy und Glencoe nach Fort William, bei Kyle of Lochalsh geht es zur Isle of Skye und damit in eine Welt für sich. Schottland ist pure Magie, manchmal beklemmende Einsamkeit, ein Wechselbad der Wetterlagen. Sonne, Nebel, Regen, dann wieder ein tiefblau leuchtender Himmel mit weißen Schäfchenwolken, die sich im Wasser der Lochs und Fjorde spiegeln. Den einschüchternden und atemberaubenden Weg über den Applecross Pass darf man sich auf keinen Fall entgehen lassen, spätestens zwischen Ullapool und Unapool hat einen der Norden kalt erwischt.

Gut, wenn man jetzt in einem Porsche Panamera 4 E-Hybrid sitzt, der trotz seiner Größe erstaunlich gut auf die winkligen, schmalen Straßen mit ihrem wettergegerbten Gesicht passt. Er ist komfortabel und schnell, wenn es über die endlosen Geraden der Hochmoore geht, fährt wie ein Berserker über die Serpentinen, kann aber auch schmeichelnd und sanft sein. Cooles Elektro-Drehmoment und mächtige V6-Power in genialer Symbiose, so vielseitig und eindringlich wie die Küstenstraße rüber nach John o'Groats und so hartnäckig wie der lange Weg bis zurück hinunter nach Inverness. Die Cairngorms werden zum abschließenden Heldenepos, das uns hilft, noch ein paar Stunden lang das Ankommen in der Normalität hinauszuschieben. Bei Edinburgh grüßen wir die Nordsee und machen dann mit einer letzten Etappe die Runde komplett. Zugegeben: Wir haben die NC500 immer wieder mal verlassen, das Landesinnere der Highlands lockt doch zu sehr, um sich strikt an den Verlauf der offiziell vom schottischen Tourismusbüro ausgeschriebenen Route zu halten. Freiheit ist hier oben inklusive. Deshalb sind wir hier.

It all starts in Glasgow. From the south, the grey city on the River Clyde stands as the western gate to the Scottish Highlands. But it's not until Loch Lomond & The Trossachs National Park that the Highlands show their teeth. The countryside is unspoilt, harsh and sombre. And you drive yourself dizzy in a rush of amazing nature, majestic landscapes and curves, curves, curves. Through Bridge of Orchy and Glencoe to Fort William, by Kyle of Lochalsh to the Isle of Skye – a world of its own. Scotland is pure magic, sometimes oppressive solitude, a constantly shifting panoply of weather. Sun, fog, rain then back to a dazzling blue sky with puffy, white cotton-wool clouds reflecting in the waters of the lochs and sea lochs. The intimidating and breathtaking road over the Pass of the Cattle to Applecross is one not to be missed. And somewhere between Ullapool and Unapool, the north has you firmly in its grasp.

It's a good thing to be sitting in a Porsche Panamera 4 E-Hybrid, which in spite of its size is ideal for the weather-beaten surface of the narrow, winding roads. It is quick and comfortable on the endless straights across the high moorland, drives like maniac through the serpentines, but can also be cajoling and gentle when need be. A glorious symbiosis of cool electric torque and mighty V6 power, as multifaceted and striking as the coast road over to John o' Groats and as tenacious as the long trek back down to Inverness.

The Cairngorms are the final heroic epic that, for a couple of hours, helps us put off the arrival back into normality. We greet the North Sea near Edinburgh and then complete the loop with a final stage. Admittedly, we left the NC500 quite a few times. The inland draw of the Highlands is way to strong to stick strictly to the official route as described by Visit Scotland. Freedom is part of the deal up here, which is why we're here.

SCHWEIZ // SWITZERLAND
ENGADIN

PORSCHE 911 GT2 RS
PORSCHE 911 ST REPSOL

PORSCHE 911 GT2 RS
PORSCHE 911 ST REPSOL

Skijöring hat im Hause Porsche Tradition, diesen Impuls nehmen wir mehr als begeistert auf. Und weil es so schön ist, wird auf dem Weg zum Sankt Moritzersee am eiskalten Berninapass warmgefahren. Driftwinkel inklusive.

Skijöring has a tradition at Porsche, we are more than enthusiastic about this idea. And because it is so beautiful, we take the ice cold Bernina Pass to warm up the engine on our way to Lake St. Moritz. Drift angle included.

Porsche 911 GT2 RS und 911 ST Repsol auf eiskalter Pass-Straße, bedeckt mit Salzstaub, passagenweise unter hereingewehtem Schnee versteckt, Schmelzwasser-Bäche folgen dem Verlauf der Straße. Und wir lassen die intensivsten Elfer ihrer jeweiligen Epoche ganz intensiv fliegen. Mächtiges Voranstürmen, haarfeiner Kampf um jeden Mikrometer Traktion, dazu ein schneeweiß glühendes Panorama das sich von den Netzhäuten bis in die Seele brennt. Aus diesem Material sind unvergessliche Momente gemacht, die in der Erinnerung später immer wie in Zeitlupe ablaufen werden. Und dann gibt es da die Zeitraffer-Erlebnisse. Wie ein paar Minuten später unten im Tal.

Skijöring, das ist diese traditionelle norwegische Wintersportart, bei der sich ein Skifahrer an einem Seil von einem Pferd, Schlittenhund oder Automobil ziehen lässt. Auch in den Alpen hat der rasante Schneesport seine Tradition: Schon Anfang des 20. Jahrhunderts ließen sich die Skifahrer von Rennpferden über den zugefrorenen Sankt Moritzsee ziehen. Auch bei den Olympischen Winterspielen von 1928 in St. Moritz war Skijöring eine offizielle Disziplin. Porsche-Nostalgikern dürfte derweil das erste Dr.-Porsche-Gedächtnis-Skijöring in Erinnerung sein, das am 10. Februar 1952 in Zell am See ausgetragen wurde. Skijöring macht riesig Spaß, aber auch im Kern einsam: Vorne will ein 700 PS-Monster oder ein auskeilender Klassikrallye-Bolide zu möglichst eleganter Form dressiert werden, hinten kämpfst du gegen Schwerkraft, Fliehkraft, schwindende Bein- und Bizepskraft. Die Skifahrer haben den Dreh raus, bleiben ganz schön lange im eiskalt strudelnden Karussell und lassen erst ganz spät ihr Seilende fliegen. Vermutlich auch nur, weil die jetzt ans Steuer wollen. Driften, Rallye-Style.

A Porsche 911 GT2 RS and a 911 ST Repsol on an ice-cold mountain pass covered with salt and grit, sections of which are completely hidden undersnow drifts, with streams swollen with melt water following the twists and turns of the road as they rush into the valley below, and we let the most power-packed 911s of their time let loose. To fly along at breakneck speed, fighting tooth and nail for every micrometre of traction, and surrounded by a spectacular snow-white panorama that burns its way through from the eyeballs deep into one's soul. This is what makes for unforgettable moments that will later be remembered as if they had happened in slow motion. And then there are moments that go by in a flash. Like the ones we experience a few minutes later down in the valley.

Skijöring is a traditional Norwegian winter sport in which a skier is pulled along by a horse, a sled dog, or an automobile. Even in the Alps, the fast-paced snow sport has its traditions – as early as the beginning of the 20th century, race horses drew skiers across the frozen lake of St. Moritz. And at the 1928 Olympic Winter Games in St. Moritz, Skijoring be-came an official sport. Porsche nostalgics might also remember the Dr Porsche memorial Skijoring, which was held in February of 1952 in Zell am See.

Skijöring is great fun, but basically you're on your own – up front, there's a 700 bhp monster or a careering classic rally car designed to move along as elegantly as possible, while coming up behind, you are fighting with the force of gravity, centrifugal force, and loss of strength in your arms and legs.

SCHWEIZ // SWITZERLAND
FRANKREICH // FRANCE
FLÜELAPASS, SUSTENPASS,
GRIMSELPASS, TREMOLA,
ROUTE DES GRANDES ALPES

19 X PORSCHE 918 SPYDER

19 X PORSCHE 918 SPYDER

Ihr sollt 19 Freunde sein – bei der epischen Alpen-Querung mit einem Rudel Porsche 918 Spyder wurden es dann am Ende doch noch mehr. Die größte Entdeckung: Freude ist dann am stärksten, wenn man sie teilt.

It was meant to be 19 friends. However, it ended up being a lot more than that on the epic Alpine crossing with a pack of Porsche 918 Spyders. The biggest discovery of all was that joy is most intense when shared.

Hypercars werden wenig gefahren und sind zu einem fahlen Schattendasein in penibel sortierten Sammler-Garagen verurteilt? – Sagen wir es einmal so: Wenn sich 19 Porsche 918 Spyder am Fuß der Alpen treffen, um dann innerhalb von 5 Tagen 25 Pässe zu absolvieren, kann kaum noch von Schonbezug-Mentalität gesprochen werden. Das Feld wird je nach individuellem Anspruch und Fahr-Rhythmus portioniert, die Stimmung ist episch, das Wetter royal und die gefahrenen Strecken endgültig. Genau so etwas nennt man bei Ausnahme-Sportwagen wie dem 918 Spyder dann wohl artgerechte Haltung. Hier wird nicht verzärtelt, gehätschelt und poliert, sondern ausgiebig Strecke gemacht.

Im Kern so einer Ausfahrt stehen zwei Elemente: die Freude an Freundschaft und Miteinander, die Freude am Fahren und an der exquisiten Technik. Der Porsche 918 Spyder ist ein mächtiges Gerät, das sichtlich Auslauf braucht. Allein der Anblick, wie sich die Maschine still Elektronen durch das neongelbe Ladekabel in die Batterie saugt, Kraft sammelt, die Muskeln spannt, lässt einen innerlich warmlaufen, und dann kommt der große Tag: frühmorgens mit summendem Elektroantrieb im Dunkeln auf die Bahn rollen, voller Erwartung den V8-Nachbrenner zünden. Es ist ein langer, einsamer Weg bis in den Süden, hinter die Berge, aber er lohnt sich. Am Ausgangspunkt der Reise setzt ein herrlicher Schock ein – es gibt sie wirklich: Menschen wie du, die sich bei Porsche dem ultimativen Traum verschrieben haben. 918 Spyder, das muss man wirklich wollen, das hat in erster Linie etwas mit der Freude an Innovation zu tun, mit einer ausgeprägten Entrücktheit und purer Leidenschaft, schließlich ist der Hybrid-Sportwagen ein Stück Zukunft im Hier und Jetzt. 918 Spyder, das ist die Freude am ultimativ technisch Machbaren, das funktioniert nur, wenn du weißt, dass allein dieses Auto deinen inneren Luke Skywalker glücklich machen kann. Und die Feststellung, dass es von deiner Sorte Minimum neunzehn gibt, ist atemberaubend. Ebenso wie die fünf Tage auf der Route des Grandes Alpes, an Susten, Flüela und Grimselpass. Königlich.

They say that hyper cars are rarely driven, and condemned to a dim, shadowy existence in the meticulously ordered garages of zealous collectors. So, let's just say this: When 19 Porsche 918 Spyders meet at the foot of the Alps to cover 25 passes in the space of five days, that's hardly what you would call a slipcover mentality. The field is laid out according to individual requirements and driving rhythm, the mood is epic, the weather fabulous and the roads definitive. It's exactly what you would call the natural habitat for an exceptional sports car such as the 918 Spyder. There's no mollycoddling here, no pampering, preening and polishing – just one-hundred percent driving.

At the heart of a trip like this are two elements: the joy of friendship and companionship, and the joy of driving and exquisite technology. The Porsche 918 Spyder is a mighty piece of machinery that clearly needs an outlet. Just the look of it, as it silently sucks electrons into its battery through the neon-yellow charging cable, gathering power, tensing its muscles, gives you a warm feeling inside. And then comes the big day: Rolling onto the road in the early-morning darkness with the electric drive humming, firing up the V8 engine in eager anticipation. It's a long, lonely road south over the mountains – but worth it. Then, at the trip's starting point, a glorious surprise: They really do exist – people like you, who committed themselves at Porsche to their ultimate dream. A 918 Spyder is something you really have to want. It has something to do with the joy of innovation, with a state of absolute trance and sheer passion. After all, this hybrid sportscar is a glimpse of the future in the here and now. A 918 Spyder is utterly absurd. It only works when you know that this car alone can make your inner Luke Skywalker happy. And the realisation that there are at least nineteen of your kind is breathtaking. Just like the five days on the Route des Grandes Alpes, on the Susten, Flüela and Grimsel passes. Heavenly.

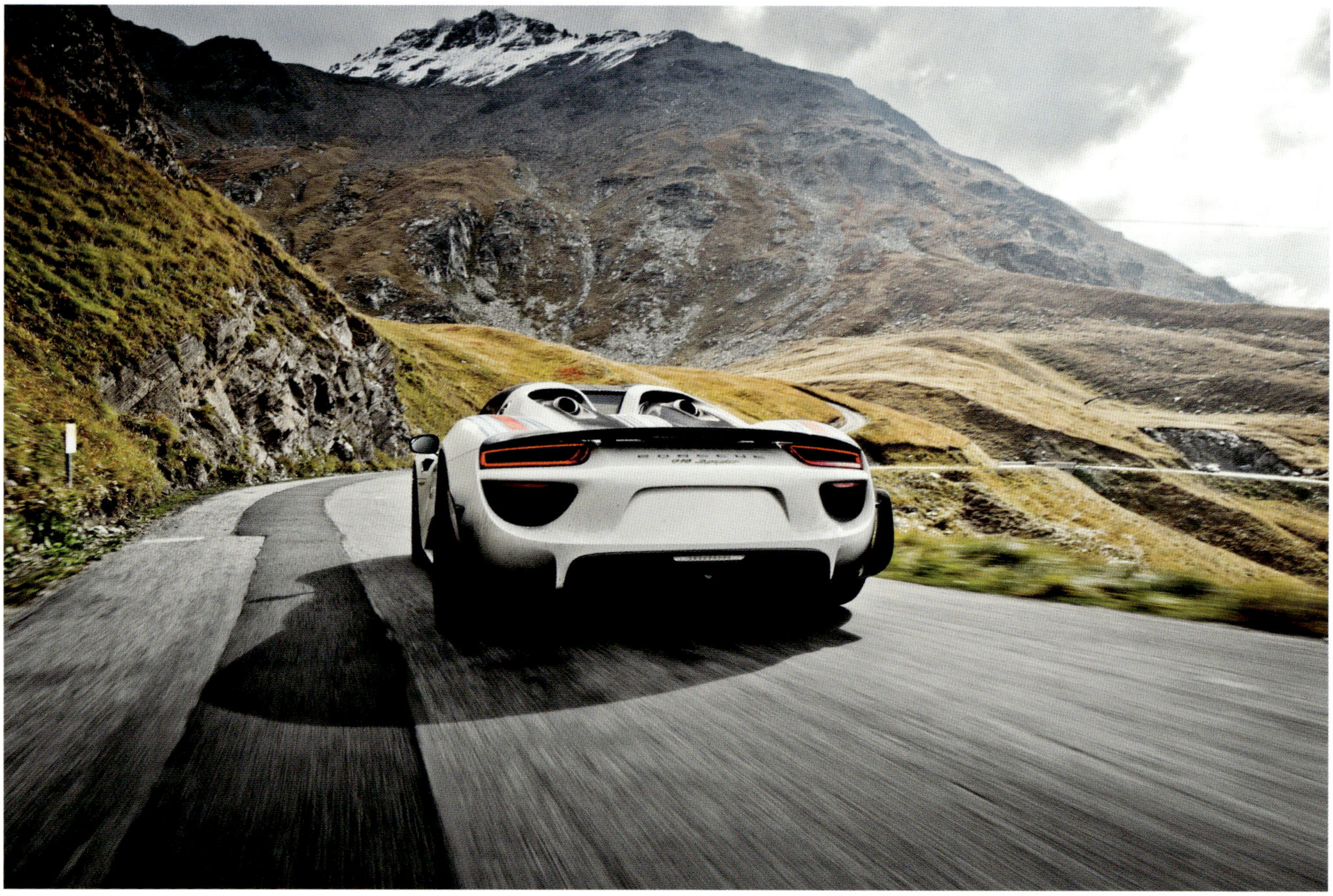

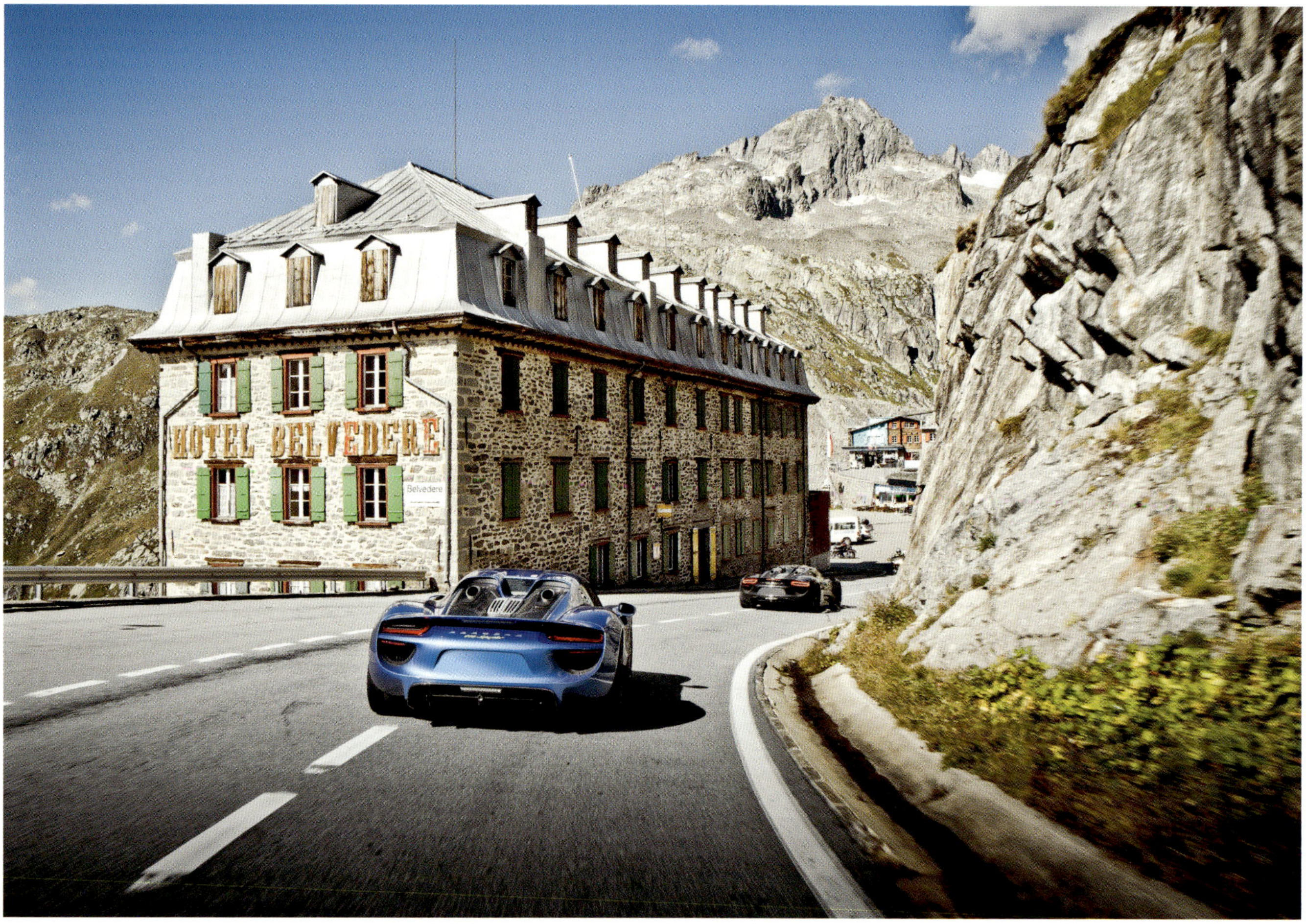
HOTEL BELVEDERE
Belvedere

CARS & CURVES SCHWEIZ – SWITZERLAND & FRANKREICH – FRANCE / 19 X PORSCHE 918 SPYDER – 143

FRANKREICH // FRANCE
ROUTE DES GRANDES ALPES

PORSCHE 914/6
PORSCHE 911 ST
PORSCHE CAYMAN GT4
PORSCHE 911 GT3 RS

PORSCHE 914/6
PORSCHE 911 ST
PORSCHE CAYMAN GT4
PORSCHE 911 GT3 RS

Intensiv. Berückend. Atemlos. 700 Kilometer über die Alpen, vom Genfer See bis ans Mittelmeer. Die Route des Grandes Alpes. Diese Strecke in extrem sportlichen Porsche zu fahren, ist herrlicher Wahnsinn.

Intense. Enthralling. Breathless. 700 kilometres over the Alps, from Lake Geneva to the Mediterranean. The Route des Grandes Alpes. Driving this road in extreme Porsches is sublime madness.

Am Anfang ist alles noch ganz einfach: mit Lärm und Wildheit losstürmen, in den Ortschaften die verwunderten Blicke genießen, pure Begeisterung kultivieren. Genfer See, dann der Col des Gets zum Aufwärmen. Drei Pässe weiter sind alle Fahrer ganz still und konzentriert geworden, denn bereits der Cormet de Roselend erreicht knapp 2000 Höhenmeter und dahinter türmt sich der Col de l'Iseran. 2764 Meter über dem Meer. Höchster Straßenpass der Alpen. Hier oben ist vor allem der Mann im Porsche 914 zur Personifikation eines strengen Gasfußes geworden. Dünne Höhenluft lässt die 110 PS des sonst dramatisch marschierenden Mittelmotor-Sportwagens ringen, im Rückspiegel drängen ein moderner Cayman GT4 sowie ein Duo aus klassischem Porsche 911 ST und aktuellem 911 GT3 RS. Schärfer geht es kaum, der 914 wird sich deshalb seine Gangart suchen: Surfen. Rhythmus. Analog.

Bald wird es auch für den ST der 1970er-Jahre eng, mit seiner kompromisslosen Racing-Auslegung sucht er nach jeder Kehre eine lange Mulsanne-Gerade, um alle 250 PS leuchten lassen zu können. Es sind schäumende, donnernde und tobende Pferde, er ist schnell, sagenhaft schnell, aber wenn ein Cayman GT4 Jäger ist, hat der alte Bolide das Nachsehen. Denn der fokussierteste Cayman aller Zeiten vergisst einfach immer wieder seinen Geheimtipp-Status. Er fährt federleicht und skalpellpräzise, hat souveräne Leistung in beinahe zart arrangierter Fahrzeugbalance, seinem Fahrer gehen Kronleuchter im Sekundenbruchteil-Takt auf: So geht Sportwagen. Aber dann klopft der Platzhirsch hinten an, der 911 GT3 RS sagt höflich: Lass mich da mal kurz vorbei. Wie er es schafft, so phänomenal schnell zu sein, selbst auf engen Passstraßen am Col du Galibier, Col d'Izoard, Col de la Cayolle und endlich am Col de Turini weit im Süden ein flammendes Bukett aus Fahrbarkeit und Energie zu entfalten, ist atemberaubend. In seinen besten Momenten wird der Fahrer zum GT3 RS. Mensch und Maschine als Überwesen. Die Route des Grandes Alpes als seelentiefes Erlebnis. Soulful Driving.

It all starts simply enough – storming off in a whirl of sound and ferocity, revelling in the looks of amazement as we pass through villages, cultivating sheer pleasure. Lake Geneva then the Col des Gets to warm up. Three passes later, all the drivers have fallen silent and fully focused as the Cormet de Roseland rises to almost 2000 metres, with the Col de l'Iseran towering behind it. 2764 metres above sea level – the highest road in the Alps. Up here, the man in the Porsche 914 has, more than any other, become the personification of a heavy right foot. Thin mountain air causes the 110 hp of the otherwise strident mid-engine sports car to struggle. Looming in the rear-view mirror are a modern Cayman GT4 as well as a classic Porsche 911 ST and a present-day 911 GT3 RS. The pressure is on and the 914 needs to find its pace – surfing, rhythm, analogue. The going soon gets tough for the ST from the 1970s. With its uncompromising racing set-up, it looks for a long Mulsanne Straight after every corner to let loose all 250 of its horses. They're frothing, thundering, riotous beasts. It's fast, fabulously fast, but when it's hunted by a Cayman GT4, the old race car is at a disadvantage. The most focused Cayman on the planet simply keeps forgetting its secret-tip status. It handles as light as a feather and with scalpel-like precision; its performance is sublime and paired with almost delicately arranged balance. The driving sensation is like a thousand light bulbs going off in rapid succession. This is what sports-car driving is all about.

But then the alpha wolf behind puts in an appearance. The 911 GT3 RS says politely: Would you mind letting me past. It's simply breathtaking how it manages to be so phenomenally fast, even on the narrow pass roads of the Col du Galibier, Col d'Izoard, Col de la Cayolle and, finally, on the Col de Turini in the far south, to deliver a flaming bouquet of razor-sharp handling and energy. In its best moments, the driver becomes the GT3 RS. Man and machine as a superbeing. The Routes des Grandes Alpes is an experience that reaches deep into the soul. Soulful driving.

CARS & CURVES	FRANKREICH – FRANCE / PORSCHE 914/6, 911 ST, CAYMAN GT4, 911 GT3 RS – 165

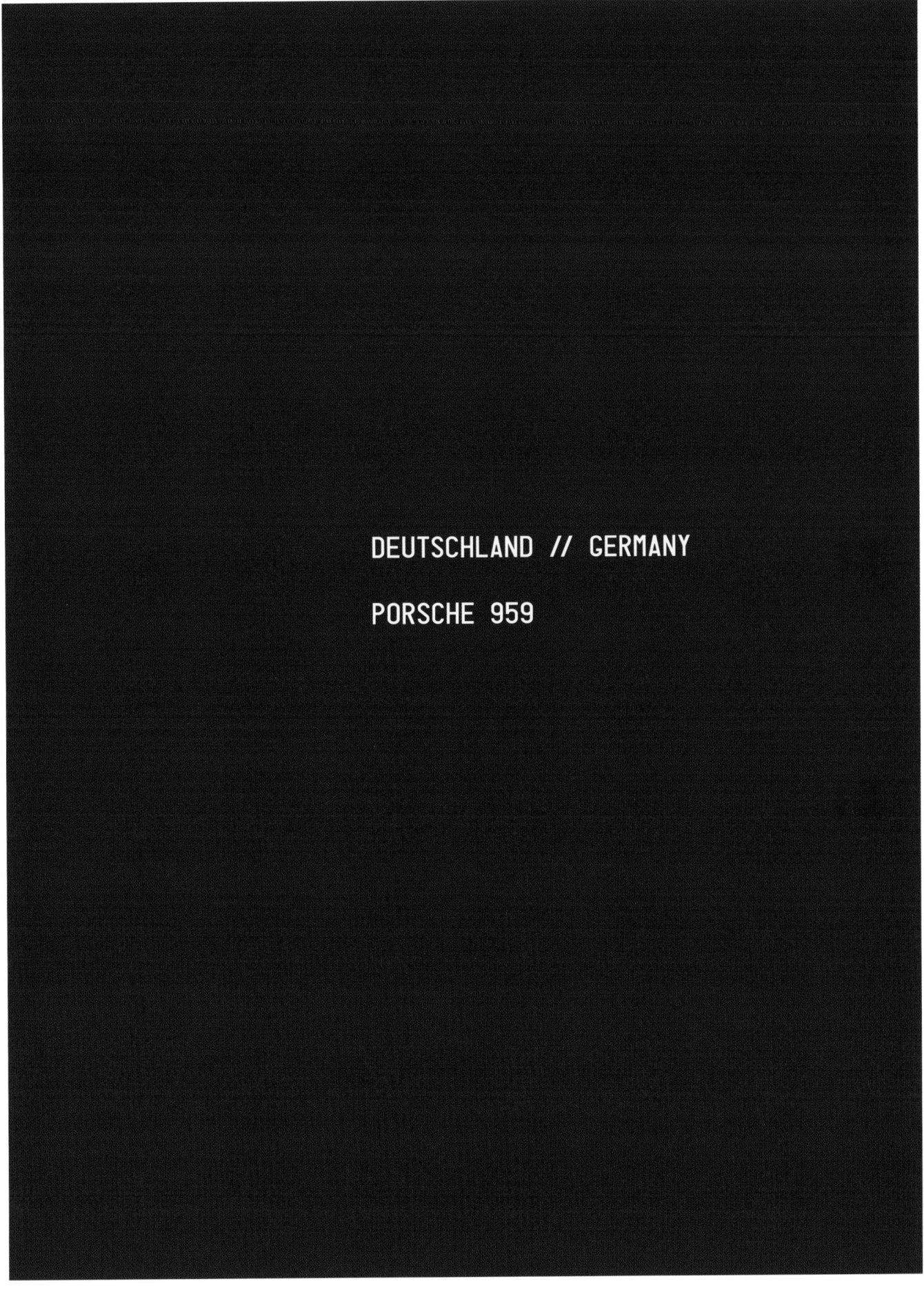

DEUTSCHLAND // GERMANY

PORSCHE 959

PORSCHE 959

Er ist das Hypercar der Eighties. Porsche 959. 450 PS-Turbo-Boxer, elektronisch geregelter Allradantrieb. Autofahren wie nach 30 Jahren die erste Episode „Star Wars" noch einmal ansehen. Und wieder Fan sein.

It's the hypercar of the Eighties – the Porsche 959. 450 hp boxer engine, electronically controlled all-wheel drive. Driving it is like watching the first episode of 'Star Wars' again after 30 years. And becoming a fan all over again.

Da steht er, der Auto-Held der 1980er-Jahre, in unverfänglichem Silber und mit diesem unverschämten Riesenbügel-Flügel am Heck. Seine Technologie führte vor drei Jahrzehnten zu Starschnitt-Postern in Automobilzeitschriften, blanko ausgestellten und bei Porsche Händlern hinterlegten Schecks sowie sprachlosen Porsche Wettbewerbern. 450 Biturbo-PS und ein elektronisch geregelter Allradantrieb waren damals beinahe Science Fiction. Drei Jahrzehnte später ist der 959 immer noch eine Legende, der englische Besitzer unseres Exemplars auf Heimaturlaub: deutscher Sportwagen in Deutschland – das muss endlich mal ausgetestet werden. Ob so ein Porsche auf Mutterboden wohl anders fährt? Die kleinen Straßen von Sussex und Kent hat der kompakte Supersportler mit dem großen Herz ganz gut drauf, aber wie ist das im Land nördlich der Alpen? Und vor allem: auf der Autobahn? Erster Gang, Klack. Kupplung wie im Fitness-Studio. Der Biturbo-Sechszylinder röchelt unruhig, dann bellt er mit präsenter mechanischer Aura los. Rundes Muskelspiel, drahtig und wach. Und dann, bei mittleren Drehzahlen, wacht das Turbo-Tier auf ... Finger auf die Fast-Forward-Taste, wie damals am Walkman. Alle Nadeln der analogen Armaturen laufen Amok, das ganze Auto verwandelt sich in pure Energie. Innerhalb von wenigen Sekunden macht sich dieses gnadenlose Speed-Eisen ganz lang, die Ohren liegen flach am Kopf, Freudentränen laufen waagerecht nach hinten aus den Augenwinkeln und das Herz schlägt einem bis zum Hals. Was für eine Kraftentladung! Den nächsten Gang kriegst du gerade noch so, aber schon zappelt der Drehzahlmesser wieder bei Rot. Nächster Gang. Und Backpfeife. Mit gewaltigem Respekt vor diesem Auto-Helden runter von der Autobahn. Die Straße turnt durch den deutschen Wald, schnörkelt in wunderschönen Radien dahin. Jetzt weckt der 959 eine Aura der Solidität und Kontrollierbarkeit, die aus dieser Epoche sehr ungewohnt scheint. Straße abtasten, Traktion feiern, mit viel Gefühl. Das ist der 959: vollkommen geerdeter Irrsinn. Was. Für. Ein. Auto.

There it is, the automotive hero of the 1980s, in innocuous silver and with this enormous, brazen wing on the rear. Three decades ago, its technology earned it collector posters in car magazines, blank checks handed in to Porsche dealers and stunned Porsche competitors. 450 twin-turbocharged hp and electronically controlled all-wheel drive were pretty much science fiction in those days. Three decades later, the 959 is still a legend. The British owner of this particular one has brought it back for a holiday in the land of its birth. A German sports car in Germany – it's high time for a test drive. Does a Porsche like this feel any different on its home turf? The compact super sports car with the big heart can handle the back roads of Sussex and Kent with ease. But what about the land north of the Alps? And above all, on the autobahn? First gear – clunk. A clutch straight out of the gym. The biturbo six-cylinder crackles restlessly, then bellows forth with a forceful mechanical aura. Well-rounded muscles flexing, taut and alert. And then, as the revs pick up, the turbo tiger awakens... finger on the fast-forward button, like a Walkman. All the needles on the analogue instruments run amok, the whole car turns into pure energy. In the space of just a few seconds, this merciless speed freak stretches flat out – your ears press back against your head, tears of joy flowing horizontally from the corners of your eyes and your heart beats out of your chest. What an explosion of power! You just about manage the next gear, but the rev needle is already hovering around red again. Next gear – and an almighty slap in the face.

With lots of respect for this automotive hero, you leave the autobahn. The road winds through the German forest in a series of glorious twists and turns. The 959 now inspires an aura of solidity and controllability that seems strange and unfamiliar from this era. Feel your way along the road, revelling in the traction, with plenty of heart and soul. That's the 959 – completely grounded insanity. What. A. Car.

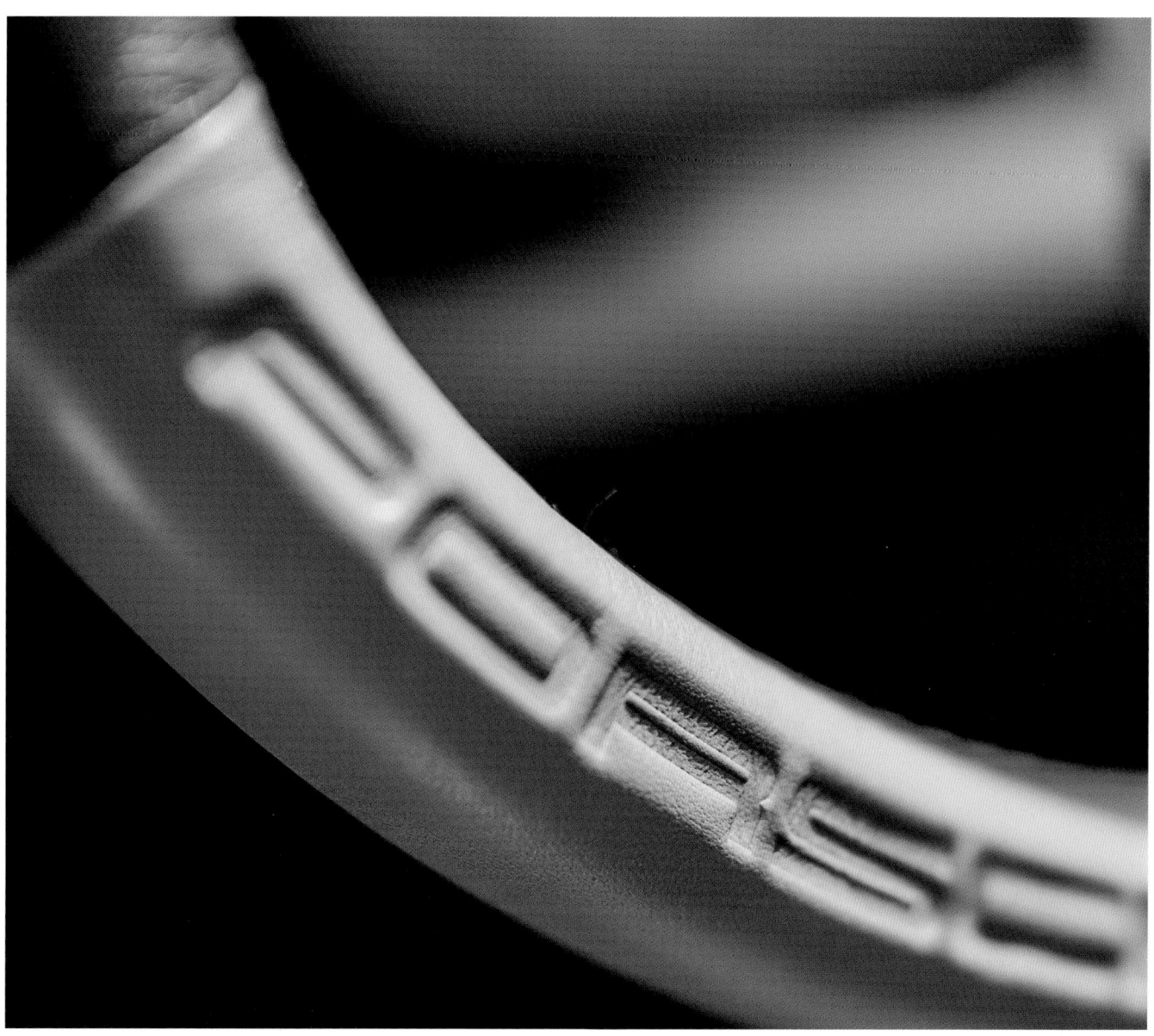

PORSCHE CAYENNE

Rund um den Norden Deutschlands, rund um Dänemark. Eine windzerzauste Küstenfahrt im biscayablauen Porsche Cayenne. Dünen und Deiche, Hamburg und Kopenhagen. Ein maritimer Tagtraum. Und immer hart am Wind.

Across the north of Germany and once around Denmark. A windblown coastal drive in a Biscay blue Porsche Cayenne. Dunes and dykes, Hamburg and Copenhagen – a maritime daydream. With a relentless headwind.

Diese Fahrt wollten wir schon lange einmal unternehmen: Deutschland hat nicht nur ein, sondern zwei Meere. Die wilde Nordsee und die milde Ostsee. Hinzu kommt: Wer die Küstenlinie Deutschlands entlangfahren will, muss zwangsweise immer auch durch Dänemark. Von der holländischen Grenze im Westen über die dänische Grenze im Norden, weiter auf die Nordsee-Inseln, hoch in den Norden und dann ans kieferngesäumte Ostseeufer mit Blick nach Polen. Kein kurzer Kurvenmoment, sondern eine Reise vor dem Wind. Und als dann der Porsche Cayenne vorbeikam, souverän, stark und mit Windeseile, war die Zeit vollkommen reif. Die Fahrt führt durch einige der am höchsten industrialisierten Gebiete Europas, hinein in die Metropolen des Nordens – gleichzeitig aber auch durch urwüchsige Natur, sprichwörtlich ans Ende der Welt. Autobahnen, mehrspurige Verkehrsadern und dann wieder schmale, grüne Sträßchen zwischen Dörfern, Feldern, Deichen. Genau richtig für die hellwache Kurven-Liebe des Cayenne, seinen Meilenfresser-Komfort und seine Emotionalität. Der Start unter Windrädern an der Nordseeküste. Die Tour durch den Hamburger Hafen, das coole und schöne Hamburg. Dann die Fahrt an der Elbe entlang zurück ans Meer. Ganz sanft auf den Strand von Sankt Peter-Ording. Am Nordstrand über die riesigen Sandflächen, die hier als Parkplatz dienen, mit Anlauf durch eine Swimming-Pool-große Pfütze gischten und das tropfende Auto dann neben die zerbeulten Camper der Kitesurfing-Gemeinde stellen. Dann Sylt, das wilde, abweisende und einladende Sylt. Rauer Wind im Strandhafer. Die Fähre hinüber nach Rømø und dann mit dem Porsche Cayenne über die Sandpisten im Süden der Insel. Mit dem Auto in den Dünen, das ist hier erlaubt. Endlich draußen sein, auf dem weiten Strand. Durch seichte Wasserrinnen fliegen, durch auslaufende Wellen spritzen, der Cayenne macht sich nass. Ein Tag am Meer. Und dann der lange Weg nach Norden, die vielen Kilometer geradeaus, während kalter Wind dicke Regentropfen auf den Porsche klatschen lässt. Kopenhagen, wunderschönes Kopenhagen, die Sonne taucht wieder auf und treibt den Porsche auf die erste Fähre des Tages nach Lübeck. Bis nach Rügen sind es jetzt nur noch wenige entspannte Stunden in reifen Kornfeldern.

We have been looking forward to this trip for a long time: Germany doesn't have just one, but two seas – the wild North Sea and the mild Baltic Sea. Added to that is the fact that, if you want to drive along Germany's coastline, you have no choice but to drive through Denmark. From the Dutch border in the west across the Danish border to the north onto the North Sea islands and further northwards, before heading for the pine-fringed shores of the Baltic with a view over to Poland. No short cornering moment, but a journey in the wind. And when the Porsche Cayenne passed by, confident, strong and fast, the time was absolutely right. The trip leads through some of Europe's most industrialised areas and into the major cities of the north – yet also through rugged, unspoiled scenery, metaphorically at the end of the world. Autobahns, multilane highways followed by narrow, green roads through villages, fields and dykes. Just right for the Cayenne's wide awake love of curves, its mile-eating comfort and its emotionality. It starts beneath wind turbines on the North Sea coast then tours through the docklands of Hamburg and the beautiful, cool city itself. Then there's the drive along the River Elbe back to the sea and very gently onto the beach at Sankt Peter-Ording. Driving on the North Beach along enormous sandflats that serve as car parks, surging through puddles the size of swimming pools then parking the dripping car next to the dented camper vans of the kitesurfing community. After that comes Sylt – wild, abrasive and inviting Sylt. Raw, biting wind in the beach grass. Take the ferry over to Rømø and drive the Porsche Cayenne along the sandy roads on the south of the island. You're allowed to take your car into the dunes here. Then, finally, out onto the endless expanse of sand, flying through shallow rivulets, kicking up spray on the edge of the waves – the Cayenne gets itself all wet. A day at the seaside. After that is the long road north – straight ahead for mile upon mile, while cold wind sends heavy raindrops splashing onto the Porsche. Copenhagen – wonderful, wonderful Copenhagen – the sun makes its reappearance and forces the Porsche onto the first ferry of the day to Lübeck. It's now just a few relaxed hours through fields of ripe corn to Rügen.

188 – PORSCHE CAYENNE / DEUTSCHLAND – GERMANY & DÄNEMARK – DENMARK

CARS & CURVES

PORSCHE CARRERA GT

Manchmal sendet das Stilfser Joch mitten in der Nacht Signale ans Unterbewusstsein: Komm vorbei, lange nicht gesehen. Drei Stunden später steht dein Porsche Carrera GT am Berg. Momente für die Ewigkeit.

Sometimes, the Stelvio Pass sends signals to your subconscious in the middle of the night: Come on over, I haven't seen you in ages. Three hours later, your Porsche Carrera GT is on the mountain. Moments for eternity.

Der Passo dello Stelvio, das Stilfser Joch, verbirgt sich hinter Bergen. Wer ihn erklimmen möchte, muss zuerst tief in die Alpen hineinfahren. Egal ob aus Norden, Süden, Osten oder Westen kommend – nie liegt der Stelvio in der ersten Reihe. Aber die weite Anreise lohnt sich, das Stilfser Joch ist ein Ereignis. Wie ein Urtier brandet die Straße gegen den Berg, zieht stetig von einer alpinen Etage in die nächste. Zuerst das grüne Tal, dann bewaldete Rampen, der Übergang durch lichte Zirbel-Felder in steilem Felsengelände, dann jenseits der Baumgrenze. Ein monumental zum Himmel aufragendes Tal zwischen Fels- und Eisriesen, bezwungen von unzähligen Serpentinen, schließlich die Passhöhe. Gefühlt: Top of the World. Und erst der Beginn einer urwüchsigen Welt unter dem Himmel.

Manchmal braucht dieses Denkmal aus Asphalt, Dynamit und Schweiß ein ganz besonderes Auto, eine ganz besondere Uhrzeit: Früh am Morgen aus dem Vinschgau ins Tal einfahren, wenn die Wiesen noch vor Tau glitzern und Kaltluftseen dem Sog der Sonne trotzen. Tief in den Schalensitzen des Carrera GT eingesaugt, die Faust an der glänzend lackierten Holzkugel des Schaltknaufs geballt. Der Hebel fräst mit zarter Reibung durch die Gassen, klack, klack, 612 PS fein portioniert, 10.000 Umdrehungen von Standgas bis Dunkelrot. Triebwerksansprache in 4K-High Definition, der V10 serviert seine ungeheure Leistung berührend sensibel. Kalligraphiefein meets Vorschlaghammer-brachial. Dazu ein Motorsound wie Katzenschnurren, Sektprickeln, Sirenen-Singen. Dass auch Fahrwerk und Lenkung dieses Über-Autos der 2000er-Jahre noch heute ganz auf Höhe der Zeit sind, ist kein Wunder. Präzise. Kontrolliert. Subtil. Man möchte einfach weinen vor Glück und Schönheit, hat einen Kloß im Hals. Und dann rollt der Carrera GT durch das Joch nach Süden, bleibt nicht stehen, links und rechts zittern die ersten Fahrradfahrer in dünnen Windjacken und vor aufkeimender Abfahrt-Ehrfurcht. Morgens am Stelvio ist jeder mit seinen Dämonen allein.

The Passo dello Stelvio is hidden among the mountains. If you want to tackle it, you first have to drive deep into the Alps. It doesn't matter whether you come from the north, south, east or west, the Stelvio is quite a trek. But the long journey there is well worth the effort because the Stelvio Pass is a true experience in itself. The road clings to the mountainside like a primeval creature, climbing relentlessly from one Alpine level to the next. First the green valley, then forested stretches followed by the transition through thinning outcrops of pine to steep rocky terrain above the tree line. A monumental cleft rearing up between giants of rock and ice, conquered by countless serpentines all the way to the pass summit. It feels like you're on top of the world, and just at the start of an untouched, pristine world beneath the heavens.

Sometimes this monument of asphalt, dynamite and sweat needs a very special car, a very special time of day. Drive into the valley from Vinschgau early in the morning, when the meadowlands are still glistening with dew and lakes of cold air stubbornly defy the pull of the sun. You're sucked down deep into the bucket seat of the Carrera GT, knuckles white as your fist grips the gleaming varnish of the wooden gear knob. The stick slides through the gate with gentle friction – clack, clack - 612 hp finely proportioned, 10,000 revs from idle to dark red. Powertrain responsiveness in 4K high definition, the V10 serves up its monstrous power with reassuring sensitivity. Calligraphic delicacy meets sledgehammer brutality. The engine sounds like a cat purring, champagne sparkling, mythical sirens singing. The suspension and steering of this übercar of the 2000s is still very much state-of-the-art – and no wonder. It's precise, controlled, subtle. It makes you want to cry with happiness at the beauty of it all; brings a lump to your throat. And then the Carrera GT rolls along the pass southwards – can't stand still. To the left and right, the first cyclists shiver in thin windbreakers and in burgeoning awe of the descent ahead. Early in the morning on the Stelvio pass, everyone is alone with their demons.

ITALIEN // ITALY
SCHWEIZ // SWITZERLAND
STILFSER JOCH - STELVIO
SAN BERNHARDINO

PORSCHE 911 GT3 RS

PORSCHE 911 GT3 RS

Stelvio-Fahrt Nummer zwei. Nach Emotion kommt Analyse. Reibungskoeffizienten, Gradzahlen, Steigungswinkel, x-Quadrat plus y-Quadrat. Und welches Auto könnte das besser als der Porsche 911 GT3 RS von 2015?

Stelvio drive number two. After emotion comes analysis. Friction coefficients, degrees, angles of incline, x-squared plus y-squared. And what car could possible do that better than the 2015 Porsche 911 GT3 RS?

Man kann sich Lieblingsstrecken auf viele verschiedene Arten nähern. Zum Beispiel so: an einem schönen Tag einen guten Lauf haben, unvergessliche Momente erleben. Das geht erstaunlich oft, und irgendwann lernt man die Strecke auch zu mögen, wenn es nicht so passt. Wenn man Geduld haben muss, Regen strömt oder Wohnmobilisten ihren ideallinienschäumenden Walter-Röhrl-Moment haben. Muss auch mal sein, klar. Wer jetzt Haltung bewahrt, zeigt: Er ist erwachsen geworden. Der Pass gehört allen, wer teilen kann, hat Freunde. Vielleicht wächst ja gerade aus solchen Momenten eine noch tiefere Bindung zum Berg. Bei uns: zum Stilfser Joch.

Aber je länger man diese Strecke fährt und sie in seinen Gedanken bewegt, desto wahrscheinlicher wird dieser eine Moment, in dem man sein Stilfser Joch vollkommen analysieren möchte, um zu verstehen, aus welchem Stoff diese 50 Kilometer wirklich gemacht sind. Benötigt wird dann ein präzise geeichtes Messinstrument – ein Porsche 911 GT3 RS. Näher als in diesem Null-Toleranz-Werkzeug kann man einer hochauflösenden Analyse nicht kommen. Der RS überträgt feinste Reibwertveränderungen, scannt die Asphalt-Korngröße im Millimeterbereich, nimmt jede Fahrbahnverwerfung ins Logbuch, bewegt sich in Kurven mit äußerster Präzision. Als hätte man dir ein Tuch von den Augen gezogen, endlich mal das Objektiv scharf gestellt und alle Linsen sauber gewischt. So klar hast du diese Strecke noch nie gesehen. Vor deinem inneren Auge entsteht ein 3D-Höhenprofil, werden Randnotizen abgelegt. Endlich hast du auch das Kleingedruckte lesen können. Und dann wechselt das Wetter. Wolken ziehen auf. Asphalt kühlt um ein halbes Grad ab. Die ganze Arbeit umsonst. Alles wird anders. Der GT3 RS könnte jetzt einfach ein zweites Szenario einlesen. Oder du hörst auf diese innere Stimme, die sagt: alles Blödsinn. Wisse, dass du nichts weißt. Einfach nach Süden weiterfahren, immer weiter durchs Engadin, bis die Ortsnamen Italienisch sprechen. Am San Bernardino bist du wieder mit Spaß bei der Sache. Das reicht. Oder?

There are all sorts of ways to get close to your favourite roads. For instance, enjoy a good run on a beautiful day, experience unforgettable moments. That happens surprisingly often and, eventually, you also learn to like the route even when it's not so perfect. When you have to be patient, it's pouring with rain or motorhome drivers have their Walter Röhrl moment right in the middle of your ideal line. It happens. And if you retain your composure under these conditions – you've made it. The pass belongs to all. People willing to share have friends. Perhaps it's these moments that give rise to an even deeper connection with the mountain. In our case – the Stelvio Pass.

But the longer your drive this road, the longer it spends in your thoughts, the more likely it becomes that this is the moment you choose to conduct an in-depth analysis of the Stelvio Pass to understand exactly what it is that this 50-kilometre stretch is actually made of. And to do this, we need a precisely calibrated measuring instrument – a Porsche 911 GT3 RS. You can't get any closer to a high-resolution analysis than in this zero-tolerance automobile. The RS transits the finest changes in surface friction, scans the grain size of the asphalt down to the millimetre level, logs every single distortion of the road surface, enters bends with maximum precision. It's like lifting a veil from your eyes, finally getting the lens into focus and wiping it clean. You've never seen this road as clearly. In our mind's eye you see a 3D altitude profile complete with margin annotations. You're finally also able to read the small print. And then the weather changes. It clouds over and the asphalt cools by half a degree. All that work for nothing. Everything changes. The GT3 could now simply log a second scenario. Or you listen to this voice inside your head saying: What a load of nonsense. You don't know anything. Just keep on driving south, on through Engadin until the village names start speaking Italian. You'll be having fun again by the time you reach San Bernardino. That'll do, right?

SCHWEIZ // SWITZERLAND
FLÜELAPASS

PORSCHE 964 RS
PORSCHE 911 R

PORSCHE 964 RS
PORSCHE 911 R

Es ist ein offenes Geheimnis: Die richtige Lackierung macht ein Auto schneller. Wir reden dabei nicht über das Gewicht der Pigmente oder die Dicke des Lackauftrags, sondern über den Farbcode 82N / LM3B, Sternrubin.

It's a well-known fact – the right paintwork makes a car faster. We're not talking here about the weight of the pigment or the thickness of the paint, but about colour code 82N / LM3B, Ruby Star.

Liebevolle Selbstironie an: Porsche Fahrer trauen sich was. Das hat überhaupt nichts mit Spätbremsen und Querbeschleunigung zu tun, sondern mit Farbe. Kaum eine andere Automarke kann sich über Fahrer freuen, die ein so unbekümmertes und unverkrampftes Verhältnis zu verwegenen, ungewöhnlichen Lackierungen haben. Das ist einerseits logisch, weil ein Porsche vollkommen objektiv betrachtet auch den ausgefallensten Farbton mit unvergleichlicher Würde trägt, andererseits aber auch ein Paradoxon: zeitlosen Autoklassiker fahren und in Sachen Farbe dann voll auf Zeitgeist setzen – dazu muss man ein Rückgrat aus Edelstahl haben, ein Selbstbewusstsein wie aus deutscher Eiche gedrechselt.

Unsere Tour von 964 RS und 911 R hat also mehr als den gemeinsamen Nenner Fahrdynamik. Das ausgeräumte Leichtbau-Sportgerät ohne zweite Sitzbank, Fensterheber oder Klimaanlage war 1991 zwar ebenso ein Traum für Porsche Puristen, wie es 25 Jahre später der 911 R mit seinem 500-PS-Motor aus dem GT3, der knackigen Handschaltung, den Pepita-Stoffsitzbezügen für die Lust am analogen Vintage-Fahrvergnügen wurde, aber dieser Fährte folgen wir nicht lange. Sondern eher zwei Neunelf-Hecks, die im knalligen Lila-Lippenstift-Farbton Sternrubin vor uns herfahren, Kilometer um Kilometer. Einmal den Flüela-Pass in der Sonderfarbe 82N / LM3B erleben, dagegen verblasst alles Andere. Unten im Tal schaut man noch vorbei, in der Auto-Normalität sind wir die Sichtung ungewöhnlich lackierter Porsche 911 durchaus gewohnt. Eine Stunde später, fest in den Anblick der vor uns elegant der Passhöhe entgegensurfenden Sternrubine, erleben wir ein Wechselbad der Gefühle. Der 964 RS ist ein Kind seiner Zeit, da geht das irgendwie, aber dass der Besitzer des ultraseltenen 911 R diese noch seltenere Sonderfarbe gelöst hat, macht uns glücklich. Entsetzt. Neugierig. Entzückt. Sprachlos. Alles nur wegen einer Farbe. Oben am Pass drucksen wir den Fahrer an. Der schmunzelt: „Ich weiß, was ihr fragen wollt." – Und? Keine Antwort. Nur dieses zufriedene Lächeln.

Affectionate self-mockery – Porsche drivers are afraid of nothing. That has absolutely nothing to do with late braking and lateral acceleration, but with colour. No other car brand can rejoice in drivers with such an unencumbered and relaxed approach to weird, foolhardy paintwork. On the one hand, this is entirely logical because, from a purely objective standpoint, a Porsche wears even the most outlandish hues with utterly incomparable dignity. On the other hand, though, it is also a paradox: To drive an automotive classic and fully embrace the Zeitgeist when it comes to colour takes nerves of steel and self-confidence carved from German oak.

Our pairing of a 964 RS and 911 R thus has more than performance as a common denominator. In 1991, the stripped-out lightweight sports machine without a rear bench, window winders or air conditioning was just as much of a dream for Porsche purists as the 911 R was 25 years later for the joy of vintage, analogue driving with its 500 hp engine from the GT3, its crisp manual gearbox and Pepita houndstooth fabric upholstery. But we don't follow this particular tack for long. Instead, what we're faced with is the rear ends of two 911s in vibrant lipstick-pink 'Ruby Star' paintwork driving in front of us – mile after mile. Once you've experienced the Flüela Pass in the special paint colour 82N / LM3B all else fades into insignificance. We take a closer look down in the valley. In everyday motoring life, we're well used to the sight of Porsche 911s painted in unusual colours. An hour later, our eyes fixed on the Ruby Star surfing elegantly towards the pass summit, we find ourselves caught in a maelstrom of contrasting emotions. The 964 RS is a product of its generation. That makes it acceptable. But that the owner of the ultra-rare 911 R selected this even rarer special paint colour makes us happy, enraged, curious, charmed, speechless. All of that just because of a colour. Up on the pass, we approach the driver. He smirks: "I know what you're trying to ask" – And? No answer, just this satisfied smile.

USA
KALIFORNIEN // CALIFORNIA
NEVADA

PORSCHE 911
CARRERA S CABRIO

PORSCHE 911 CARRERA S CABRIO

Dies ist die Reise schlechthin – die Mutter aller Roadmovies. Eine epische Fahrt durch einen Traum voller schwerer Musik und süßem Weltschmerz. Im Porsche 911 Cabriolet durch Kalifornien. Noch Fragen?

This has to be the ultimate journey – the mother of all road movies. An epic drive through a dream filled with heavy music and sweet melancholy. A trip through California in a Porsche 911 Cabriolet. Any questions?

Los Angeles atmet schwer, Hitze kriecht in die Canyons, wird von den Bergen im Norden eingekesselt. Der offene 911 faucht über die Highways, tanzt im Rhythmus der Betonplattenabsätze, Hip-Hop in Inglewood, dann Latino Beats. Irgendwas mit „Corazón", das ist anscheinend wichtig. Oben in Santa Monica wartet der Pacific Coast Highway, eine kühle Brise treibt den 911 nach Norden. Warum eigentlich hat man im Cabrio am Meer immer dieses Yacht-Gefühl? Und ein Lächeln, das chronisch wird? – Bis Santa Barbara ist die Straße breit und mehrspurig, rechts die Los-Padres-Berge mit ihrer trockenen Hitze unter azurblauem Himmel, hier unten ballt sich Salz und schwüler, feuchter Wind in der Ebene am Meer. Der Fels bei Morro Bay ist ein Start für den langen Weg nach Norden, Kurven am Ozean, links der Pazifik. Eiskalte Ferne im Dunst.

Man fährt einfach so. Nirgendwo auf der Welt fährt man einfach so, nur hier. 150 Meilen Tagtraum. Eyes Wide Open. Rund um die Monterey Bay wird es etwas hektischer, ab Santa Cruz haben wir wieder Ruhepuls. Surfin' USA, der Porsche lässt seinen Sechszylinder-Boxermotor knurren, dieser Soundtrack ist beinahe besser als V8-Donner. Elegant, rauchig, Versprechen statt Drohung. Dass man dann plötzlich über die Golden Gate-Bridge rollt, kommt wie ein wunderschöner Schock.

Herzflattern hoch oben über dem Meer, rechts unten leuchtet San Francisco im Sonnenuntergang. Eine Nacht später sind wir bereits wieder weit entfernt, der Pazifik ist eine bloße Erinnerung. Vor uns die Berge, Yosemite-mächtig, Granit-stark, Puma-wild. Und dahinter ein Albtraum aus Hitze, Stein und Ewigkeit. Tal des Todes. Alles klar? Im Porsche 911 Cabrio tun wir einfach so, als ginge uns das alles nichts an, wir fahren mittendurch. Inhalieren staubtrockene Hitze, lassen rollenden Tumbleweed-Büschen die Vorfahrt und schauen dann doch noch in Las Vegas vorbei. Dieses Mal, das letzte Mal. Versprochen.

Los Angeles is breathing heavily, heat creeps into the canyons, closed in by the mountains to the north. The open-top 911 tears along the highways, dancing to the rhythm of the concrete slabs – hip-hop in Inglewood followed by Latino beats. Something with "Corazón" – which appears to be important. Waiting up in Santa Monica is the Pacific Coast Highway; a cool breeze drives the 911 northwards. Why do you always have this yacht feeling when you drive a cabrio by the ocean? And a smile fixed firmly to your face? The road is wide and multilane as far as Santa Barbara. To the right are the Los Padres Mountains with their dry heat spread out beneath an azure sky. Down here on the plains along the seaboard, salt permeates the humid, sticky air. The rock by Morrow Bay is the starting point for the long road north. Curves at the ocean. To the left, the Pacific – its icy-cold expanse dissolving in the haze.

You just drive. Nowhere else in the world do you just drive – only here. A 150-mile daydream – eyes wide open. It all gets a bit more hectic around Monterey Bay, but resting heartrate is restored once we reach Santa Cruz. Surfin' USA – the Porsche lets its six-cylinder boxer motor hum along. This soundtrack is almost better than the V8 thunder. Elegant and smoky – promise replaces threat. It comes as a wonderful shock when we suddenly find ourselves rolling over the Golden Gate Bridge.

Our hearts flutter high up above the ocean while San Francisco gleams in the sunset off to the right below us. The next night, we're already far away again – the Pacific a mere memory. Ahead are the mountains – mighty as Yosemite, hard as granite, wild as pumas. And beyond them, a nightmare of heat, stone and eternity. Death Valley. All fine? In the Porsche 911 Cabrio, we act like it has nothing to do with us. We simply drive on through, inhaling bone-dry heat, giving way to tumbleweed and then looking in on Las Vegas on the way past. This is the very last time – promise.

ITALIEN // ITALY
STILFSER JOCH
STELVIO PASS

PORSCHE 356 CARRERA

PORSCHE 356 CARRERA

Stelvio Nummer drei. Im Porsche 356 Carrera das Stilfser Joch ins Engadin zu überqueren, ist eine exklusive Zeitreise. Auf der Königswelle bei Kaiserwetter bis zur Passhöhe. Fahren in längst vergessener Intensität.

Stelvio number three. Crossing the Stelvio Pass into the Engadin in a Porsche 356 is an exclusive journey back in time. Powered up the pass in heavenly weather by the divine Furhmann engine, this is driving of an intensity long forgotten.

Am Bella Vista Hotel in Trafoi realisierst du, dass das jetzt wirklich passiert: runterschalten, aus dem Heck prasselt der 130 PS starke Vierzylinder-Boxermotor, gefühlvoll einlenken. Dann die erste Kehre auf dem langen Weg zum Stilfser Joch. Die rot lackierte Nase des 356 schwenkt in den Radius, der kleine Sportwagen macht kurzen Prozess. Kurz blitzen Sonnenstrahlen über die Kotflügel und Chromleisten voraus, dann erklärt dir der Carrera beim Herausbeschleunigen, warum er definitiv kein Käfer ist. Statt brav ziehenden Volkswagen-Temperaments gibt es hier im Drehzahlkeller einen schlanken Fuß. Dann schnappt der nach allen Regeln der Verbrennungsmotor-Magie angefütterte Boxermotor aber zu. Öl auf Betriebstemperatur, alles auf Grün, Drosselklappen aufziehen. Es folgt: packende Leistungsentfaltung, bellender Sound. Der Carrera will rennen.

Schalten mit Zwischengas und weiter. Die Spitzkehren einen guten Kilometer weiter werden zum Fest, der 356 turnt energisch gegen den Berg an, als Fahrer bleibt einem da nur, am eigenen Stil zu arbeiten. Präzise passende Schaltpunkte, reinhören in den Motor, den richtigen Moment der Leistungscharakteristik abwarten. Den richtigen Gang hast du am besten vor der Kehre, der 356 Carrera B ist reifer als die Modelle der ersten Serie, darf aber trotzdem mit Gefühl und Engagement gefahren werden. Und bremsen, Schwung dosieren – all das will sitzen. Der 356 Carrera 2 hat längst schon nicht mehr die Trommelbremsen früherer Varianten und sein Königswellen-Boxer steht gut im Futter, aber er ist genau wie das Stilfser Joch eine Aufgabe für Fortgeschrittene, zusammen sind sie unerbittlich: Nachlässige Fahrer verzweifeln an dieser Straße, sie landen klein und schwitzend oben auf 2757 Metern, verstehen die Welt nicht mehr und kommen nie wieder. Nur Fahrer, die im 356 den Flow entfesseln, sind Könige. Und deshalb: Köpfchen beim Fahren. Dann wird alles wunderschön. Die Berge grüßen aus endlosem Blau, nicken dir huldvoll zu. Heute ist dein Tag. Königswelle bei Kaiserwetter.

At the bella Vista Hotel in Trafoi, you realise that this is actually happening. You shift down a gear, the 130 hp four-cylinder boxer engine crackles from the back, then you savour the moment as you turn in. You reach the first bend on the long road to the Stelvio Pass. The red nose of the 356 swings into the radius; the little sports car makes short work of it. Rays of sunshine dance briefly across the wings and chrome trim before the Carrera explains to you, as it accelerates out, exactly why it's definitely not a Beetle. Instead of pulling dutifully in true Volkswagen style, it shirks its responsibilities at the bottom of the rev range. But all the laws of engine magic have been applied to sweetening this boxer motor and it quickly takes the bait. The oil reaches operating temperature and it's raring to go. Throttles open, and there you have it – phenomenal power delivery, an almighty sound. The Carrera is ready to race.

You double-declutch as you shift and power onward. The hairpins up ahead are a feast for the senses, the 356 turning energetically against the mountain. As a driver, all that remains is to work on your own style. Precisely matched shift points, listening to the engine, waiting for the right moment on the power curve. It's best to be in the right gear before you enter the bend. The 356 Carrera B is more mature than the models from the first series, but can nevertheless be driven with feeling and commitment. And brake, meter out the momentum – easy does it. Although the 356 Carrera 2 no longer has the drum brakes of earlier variants, and its Fuhrmann boxer is well fed, it is nevertheless like the Stelvio Pass – a job for advanced drivers. Together, they are utterly unrelenting. Inattentive drivers despair on this road, ending up at 2757 metres a sweaty shadow of their former selves, doubting their perception of the world and swearing never to return. Only drivers able to unleash the flow in the 356 are kings. So, keep your wits about you and all will be wonderful. The mountains greet you from the infinite blue yonder, nodding benevolently. Today is your day. The divine Fuhrmann in heavenly weather.

DEUTSCHLAND // GERMANY
NÜRBURGRING

PORSCHE 956/007
PORSCHE 918 SPYDER

PORSCHE 956/007
PORSCHE 918 SPYDER

Manche Träume sind unerreichbar. Die Nürburgring-Rekordhalter Porsche 956 und 918 Spyder zusammen auf der Nordschleife, die Helden aus zwei Epochen im Formationsflug. Und dann passiert es tatsächlich.

Some dreams are simply unattainable. Two Nürburgring record holders – the Porsche 956 and 918 Spyder – together on the Nordschleife. The heroes of two eras flying in close formation. And then suddenly it happens.

Sechs Minuten und 11,13 Sekunden. Exakt so lange braucht Stefan Bellof am 28. Mai 1983, um mit seinem Porsche 956 die vielleicht für immer schnellste Rundenzeit auf der Nürburgring-Nordschleife hinzubrennen. Durchschnittsgeschwindigkeit von über 200 km/h – auch das ist bis heute ungebrochener Rekord. Der 630 PS starke Gruppe C-Rennwagen ist damit seit mittlerweile 35 Jahren ungeschlagen. Er wird zur Legende. Zur Sagengestalt. König Arthur, Ritter der Tafelrunde. Irgendwann weiß man nicht mehr so recht, ob es dieses Auto überhaupt noch gibt.

Dreißig Jahre nach Bellofs Rekordrunde taucht am Nürburgring ein 956 in Rothmans-Livrée und mit Startnummer 2 auf, wir sind wie paralysiert. Ist das …? Kopfnicken. Er ist es. Chassis-Nummer 007, das Bellof-Auto. Eine Welle der Begeisterung spült am nächsten Morgen den 956 an die Startlinie, die deutsche Rennlegende Hans-Joachim „Strietzel" Stuck wird den 956 noch einmal über die Nürburgring-Nordschleife bewegen. Und der alte Platzhirsch hat einen jungen Bewunderer im Schlepptau: Am 4. September 2013 hat der Porsche Werksfahrer Marc Lieb im Porsche 918 Spyder einen neuen, sagenhaften Rundenrekord für straßenzugelassene Serienfahrzeuge eingestellt – 6:58 Minuten, unvorstellbar. Nebel wabert über die Strecke, das mächtige, rohe Hämmern des Sechszylinder-Turbo-Boxermotors im 956 treibt die Spannung ins Unermessliche, nebenan läuft der V8 im neuen Hybrid-Supersportwagen warm. Und dann beginnt der Walküren-Ritt. Nebelfetzen werden von golden glühender Herbst-Morgensonne zerfasert, die beiden Porsche hechten in elegantem Schwung auf die Strecke. Hatzenbach, Flugplatz, Schwedenkreuz. Dicht hintereinander die Fuchsröhre hinunter, volle Konzentration am Adenauer Forst. Wie in Trance geht es über Wehrseifen zum schnellen Bergaufabschnitt Kesselchen – hier schlägt die Stunde überstarker Motoren und mutiger Fahrer. Karussell, dann die vertrackten Ecken bis zum Pflanzgarten. Auf der langen Gerade an der Döttinger Höhe hat uns der Eifel-Nebel wieder. Vielleicht war ja doch alles nur ein Traum.

Six minutes and 11.13 seconds. That's exactly how long Stefan Bellof took on 28 May 1983 to blast around the Nürburgring-Nordschleife with his Porsche 956 in what will perhaps forever remain the fastest lap time ever. An average speed of more than 200 km/h – another record unbroken to this day. The 630 hp Group C race car has remained unbeaten for the last 35 years. It has become legend. A fable. King Arthur and the Knights of the Round Table. At some point, you're not entirely sure whether this car even exists.

Thirty years after Bellof's record-breaking lap, a 956 shows up at the Nürburgring in Rothmans livery and bearing the number 2. It's like we're paralysed. Is that …? A nod of the head. It is. Chassis number 007, the Bellof car. The next morning, a wave of excitement washes over the 956 on the starting line. German racing legend Hans-Joachim "Strietzel" Stuck is going to take the 956 around the Nürburgring-Nordschleife one more time. And the old dog has a young admirer in tow. On 4 September 2013, Porsche works driver, Marc Lieb, set a new, legendary lap record for street-legal production sports cars – 6:58 minutes. Amazing. Fog wafts across the track.

The mighty, raw hammering of the six-cylinder turbo-charged boxer engine in the 956 sends the tension off the scale. Alongside it, the V8 in the new hybrid super sports car is warming up. And then the ride of the Valkyries begins. Misty strands are frayed by the golden glow of autumnal morning sun; the two Porsches sweep onto the track in an elegant arc. Hatzenbach, Flugplatz, Schwedenkreuz – one after the other then down the Fuchsröhre and 100-percent concentration at Adenauer Forst. As if in a trance over Wehrseifen to the fast uphill Kesselchen section – where the bell tolls for overpowered engines and bold drivers. Karussel, then the tricky corners leading to Pflanzgarten. The Eifel fog catches up with us again on the long straight at Döttinger Höhe. Maybe it was all just a dream after all.

278 - PORSCHE 956/007 - PORSCHE 918 SPYDER / DEUTSCHLAND - GERMANY

CARS & CURVES

ÖSTERREICH // AUSTRIA
RED BULL RING

PORSCHE TYP 64
BERLIN-ROM-WAGEN

PORSCHE TYP 64 BERLIN-ROM-WAGEN

Eine 190-km/h-schnelle Erinnerung an den Ursprung der Porsche Idee vor mehr als 70 Jahren: Der geheimnisvolle Berlin-Rom-Wagen von 1939 ist ein Kind seiner Zeit, martialisch, aerodynamisch und verwegen.

A 190 km/h memory of the origin of the Porsche idea from more than 70 years ago. The mysterious Berlin-Rome car from 1939 is a product of its generation, militaristic, aerodynamic and bold.

Und was war in der Zeit, bevor Porsche zur Marke wurde? Gehört zu einer Erinnerung an 70 Jahre Porsche nicht auch die Zeit davor? – In den 1930er-Jahren ist alles offen, automobiltechnisch wird kaum eine Idee ausgelassen, die Ingenieure scheuen auch vor den wildesten Konstruktionen nicht zurück. Das Konstruktionsbüro Porsche experimentiert für einen Langstrecken-Rennwagen mit Prototypen des späteren Volkswagen, wechselt auf eine Mittelmotor-Konfiguration mit vor der Hinterachse positioniertem, gebläsegekühltem 1,1-Liter-Boxermotor, das Getriebe landet im Heck, der Pilot wird mittig im Fahrzeug untergebracht. Wesentlicher Unterschied zum Ur-Käfer ist aber die kompromisslos aerodynamisch ausgeführte Karosserie aus gedengeltem Aluminium – Stromlinie ist in den 1930er-Jahren einfach sagenhaft modern. Schmaler Cockpit-Aufbau, flache Silhouette, Radhäuser mit Abdeckungen, die vorn bei starkem Lenkausschlag durch die Räder nach außen gedrückt werden können. Theoretisch reichen die 40 PS des Motors so für 190 km/h.

Dann bricht der Zweite Weltkrieg aus. Das Langstrecken-Rennen von Berlin nach Rom, für das dieser spektakuläre Rennwagen konzipiert wurde, hat nie stattgefunden, zwei der drei gebauten Exemplare des „Typ 64" verschwinden, ihr Verbleib ist bis heute nicht nachvollziehbar. Erst 1949 kauft der österreichische Rennfahrer Otto Mathé den letzten Stromlinien-Wagen. Über 45 Jahre ist das Auto in Mathés Besitz, wird stark modifiziert und genutzt, dann schafft es der Porsche Spezialist Michael Barbach, den Berlin-Rom-Wagen in seinen ursprünglichen Zustand zurückzuversetzen. 2008 macht sich Barbach schließlich an die Entwicklung eines eigenen Nachbaus des allerersten Berlin-Rom-Wagens: Die Karosserie wird von Hand gedengelt, Scheiben gebogen, viele Kleinteile aufwendig nachgebaut. 9.000 Arbeitsstunden später ist die Replik gelungen, im Mai 2014 fährt der Wagen zum ersten Mal. Mit einer geschwungenen Silhouette, aus der 1948 der Porsche 356, 1963 der Porsche 911 hervorgehen werden.

And what about life when Porsche was not yet a brand? In remembering the last 70 years, shouldn't we reflect on the time before? Anything was possible in the 1930s. Automotive technology was in its ascendancy and engineers were afraid of nothing. The Porsche design office was experimenting with prototypes of what would later become the Volkswagen. The goal was to create a long-distance race car. They changed the layout to a mid-engine configuration with a fan-cooled 1.1-litre boxer motor mounted in front of the rear axle. The transmission ended up in the back and the driver was put in the middle of the vehicle. The main difference to the Ur-Beetle, however, was the uncompromisingly aerodynamic bodyshell design made from panel-beaten aluminium. Streamlining was absolutely state-of-the-art in the 1930s. A narrow cockpit lid, flat silhouette, covered wheel arches that could be pushed outward at the front under heavy steering. In theory, the engine 40 hp was sufficient for 190 km/h.

Then came the outbreak of World War II and the Berlin-Rome long-distance race, for which this spectacular race car was built, never took place. Two of the three "Type 64s" disappeared, their whereabouts remaining uncertain to this day. It wasn't until 1949 that Austrian racing driver, Otto Mathé, bought the last streamline car. The car spent more than 45 years in Mathé's possession, during which it was extensively modified and used. Then Porsche specialist Michael Barbach managed to restore the Berlin-Rome car to its original state. In 2008, Barbach finally set about developing his own replica of the very first Berlin-Rome car – the bodyshell was hand beaten, window glass curved and many small parts remanufactured from scratch in painstaking detail. 9,000 man-hours later, the replica was completed and, in May 2014, the car drove for the first time, bearing the sweeping silhouette that gave birth to the Porsche 356 in 1948 and the Porsche 911 in 1963.

ISLAND // ICELAND
RING ROAD
WESTFJORDS

PORSCHE MACAN S

PORSCHE MACAN S

Wer hinter Reykjavík den Hringvegur im Uhrzeigersinn nimmt, landet im wilden Nordwesten Islands. Straßen aus schwarzem Lava-Schotter, von Feuer und Eis modelliertes Land – eine Welt an den Fjorden.

If you drive clockwise around the Hringvegur outside Reykjavík, you end up in Iceland's wild northwest. Roads of black lava gravel; a land sculpted from fire and ice – a world at the fjords.

Vierspurig über die Hügel am Stadtrand von Reykjavík. Normalität aus Kleinindustrie und Wohngebieten. Wie das täuschen kann. Wenige Minuten später ist die ganz Island umspannende Ringstraße Hringvegur nur noch ein schmales Asphaltband, das unbeirrt durch karges Land nach Norden strebt. 100 Kilometer später erwachen wir für einen kurzen Moment aus dem meilenfressenden Trott, wechseln auf die Nationalstraße 60 und schalten dann den inneren Autopiloten erneut auf Cruise-Mode. Plötzlich zieht sich eine von Bruchgeröll gesäumte Deichstraße über den ersten Meeresarm – links rollt der Nordatlantik in die Bucht, rechts lagern sich schneebedeckte Hügel. Willkommen im Vestfirðir, dem Land der Westfjorde. Verzweifeltes Gras und depressive Flechten klammern sich an Geröllwiesen und Felsen, eine ätherische Ästhetik täuscht in dieser irritierend schönen Wüste Freundlichkeit vor. In Wirklichkeit aber ist dieses Land ein Duldungsbestand der Natur des Nordens. Gemacht aus Vulkanen, verwaltet vom Wind und bedroht vom Meer. Man darf hier sein. Mehr nicht. Aber man will es. Von einer Bucht in die nächste irrlichtern, eine abstruse Mischung aus Fahrt und Stillstand. Der Porsche Macan S zieht mit in den Radhäusern trommelndem Schotter-Stakkato über die schwarzen Straßen, wenn sich plötzlich Sturzbäche vor uns ergießen, prescht er beherzt hindurch. Im nächsten Moment kommt einem das aber so endlos, bodenlos vor, dass man nicht anders kann, als zu stoppen und eine halbe Stunde verträumt durchs Geröll zu stolpern. Dann scheint der weiße SUV plötzlich aus der Ferne zu rufen: Komm, weiter. Es gibt noch so viel zu entdecken. Du hast ja mich. Er hat recht. Eine Bucht weiter spiegelt sich ein vollkommener Berg in vollkommener Wasseroberfläche. Raumschiffe landen in dampfenden Ebenen, Aliens winken. Trolle heben moosige Köpfe. Elfen huschen hinter Steine. In den Hügeln tanzen die Götter, auf den Wellen des Meeres Drachenboote. Dann kommt eine sternklare Nacht. 3500km später und die Insel umrundet sind wir in Reykjavík zurück. Und fragen uns, ob das der eigentliche Traum ist.

Four lanes lead over the hills on the outskirts of Reykjavík, flanked by the normality of small-scale industry and residential areas. Somehow disappointing. A few minutes later, the Hringvegur ring road that goes all the way round Iceland is nothing more than a narrow strip of asphalt, forging resolutely northwards through barren countryside. 100 kilometres later, we awake for a brief moment from the mile-munching trot, switch to Route 60 then re-engage the cruise mode in our inner autopilots. Suddenly a road lined with broken boulders rises up over the first inlet – to the left, the North Atlantic rolls inland; to the right, snow-covered hills. Welcome to Vestfirðir, the land of the West Fjords. Desperate grass and depressive lichen cling to the scree and rocks. An ethereal aesthetic feigns kindliness in this irritatingly beautiful desert. In reality, however, the very existence of this country is due only the acquiescence of the forces of northern nature. Forged from volcanoes, managed by wind and threatened by the sea. Man is merely permitted to be here – no more than that. But man wants to be – flitting from one fjord to the next, an absurd mixture of driving and standstill. The Porsche Macan S makes its way long the black roads to the staccato beat of gravel drumming in its wheel arches. When torrential streams gush suddenly in front of us, it dashes valiantly on through. The next moment, it all looks so endless, fathomless, that all you can do is stop and stumble dazed through the boulders. Then suddenly, the white SUV seems to be calling you from far away: Come back, there's still so much to discover. You have me. And it's right. One fjord further, an entire mountain is reflected in an entire water surface. Spaceships land on steaming plateaus, aliens wave. Trolls raise their mossy heads. Elves scurry behind stones. The gods dance in the hills while dragon boats dance on the waves out to sea. After 3500 kilometres and a complete tour of the the island, we're back in Reykjavík, asking ourselves if it isn't all just a dream.

SCHWEIZ // SWITZERLAND
SUSTENPASS, NUFENENPASS

PORSCHE 906
PORSCHE 918 SPYDER

PORSCHE 906
PORSCHE 918 SPYDER

Endgültige Sportwagen-Wunder im Herz der Alpen. Eine Runde über das Kopfsteinpflaster am Sankt Gotthard, die Kurven am Nufenenpass, die Majestät des Grimselpasses. Und dann dieser eine Moment am Susten.

Ultimate sports car heaven in the heart of the Alps. A lap on the paving stones on the St. Gotthard, the bends of the Nufenen Pass, the majesty of the Grimsel Pass. And then this one moment on the Susten.

Für einen Moment sehen wir uns in den Augen der anderen: Eine kleine Gruppe von Touristen steht auf der Aussichtsterrasse des Sustenpass-Hospiz und schaut zu uns herunter. Zwei mit der Straße verwachsene Sportwagen, die in der Sonne schimmernd dahingleiten. Diese Mischung von Fassungslosigkeit, Unglaube und Begeisterung in den Blicken. Sie müssen das stählerne Bellen des Porsche 906 gehört haben, seitdem der auf der Nordostseite in den kurzen Tunnel an der Passhöhe eingefahren ist. Sechszylinder-Boxermotoren mit diesem kernigen, atemlosen Racing-Timbre sind selten. Und in den allerseltensten Fällen auf 2200 Metern Höhe unterwegs.

Man wartet also gespannt und rechnet mit so einigem. Aber nicht mit einem reinrassigen Rennwagen der 1960er-Jahre, schneeweiß und himmelblau, mächtigen Radhäusern, luftiger Pilotenkanzel, komplettem Startnummern-Ornat. Wenn der dann aus dem Tunnel ins Freie sprengt, weiten sich die Pupillen und die Münder stehen offen. Vollkommene Verwirrung entsteht allerdings einige Sekunden später. Den im Elektro-Modus dicht dahinter durch den Tunnel flüsternden Porsche 918 Spyder hat niemand gehört, noch weniger aber erwartet. Und die Mischung aus Vintage gefolgt von Ultramoderne versetzt alle in eine Zeitblase, in einen sprachlosen, ewigen Moment.

In genau diesem Zustand sind wir seit dem Morgen unterwegs, auf einer der mächtigen Alpenrouten: Grimselpass, Nufenenpass, Sankt Gotthard und nun der Susten zurück ins Berner Oberland. Man kann diese Strecke an einem Tag schaffen, ganz versunken ins Fahren, abgetaucht in die Kurven, in die Berge. Die Strecke ist an jedem anderen Tag ein kleines Wunder für sich, heute aber – am Steuer dieser Autolegenden – ist sie ein unvergessliches Juwel. Auch der 906 und sein so viel jüngerer Bruder scheinen das zu spüren. Sie laufen makellos. Inspirierend und seelenvoll. Ein Ritt aus purer Perfektion ist das. Herrliche Eleganz, alles im Fluss. Manche Erinnerungen bleiben ein Leben lang. Wie dieser Moment oben am Sustenpass.

For a moment, we see ourselves through the eyes of others – a small group of tourists is looking down on us from the viewing terrace of the Hospiz restaurant on the Susten Pass. Two sports cars at one with the road as they glide along, shimmering in the sun. On their faces is a mixture of bewilderment, disbelief and amazement. They must have been able to hear the steely bellow of the Porsche 906 since it drove into the north side of the short tunnel at the pass summit. Six-cylinder boxer motors with this throaty, breathless racing timbre are rare. And extremely rare indeed at an altitude of 2200 metres.

So they wait, intrigued, and expect something impressive. But certainly not a thoroughbred race car from the 1960s, in snow white and sky blue, with huge wheel arches, open cockpit and a full set of racing numbers. When it then bursts out of the tunnel and into the open air, eyes widen and mouths gape. However, complete confusion doesn't occur until a few seconds later. The Porsche 918 Spyder whispering through the tunnel in electric mode has been heard by nobody and expected by none. And the mixture of vintage followed by ultra-modern sends everyone into a time warp, into a speechless, eternal moment.

And this has been exactly our state of being since we set off that morning – on one of the mighty Alpine routes: Grimsel Pass, Nufenen Pass, St. Gotthard and now the Susten back to the Berner Oberland. You can do this route in one day, totally lost in driving, absorbed by the curves, by the mountains. On any day, this route is a small wonder in its own right, but today – at the wheel of these automotive legends – it's an unforgettable jewel. The 906 and its much younger brother seem to sense that, too. They run flawlessly – inspiring and soulful. It is a ride of sheer perfection, stunning elegance, where everything flows. Some memories stay with you for a lifetime – this moment on the Susten Pass is one of them.

328 - PORSCHE 906 - PORSCHE 918 SPYDER / SCHWEIZ - SWITZERLAND

CARS & CURVES

ÖSTERREICH // AUSTRIA
RED BULL RING
ITALIEN // ITALY
STILFSER JOCH
STELVIO PASS

PORSCHE 911 ST REPSOL

PORSCHE 911 ST REPSOL

Diese Rarität der 911er-Ahnenreihe ist Rennstreckentier durch und durch. 45 Jahre alte Erfolge machen den äußerst seltenen Porsche 911 ST zur Legende. Aber manchmal will er einfach nur spielen.

This rarity in the 911 bloodline is a racetrack beast through and through. Success 45 years ago make this extremely rare Porsche 911 ST a legend. But sometimes, all it wants to do is play.

Anfang der 1970er-Jahre fertigt die Porsche Rennabteilung eine ausgesprochene Rarität: Der für Langstrecken- und Rallye-Einsätze gedachte 911 ST wird durch seine Seltenheit und Rennerfolge zum Mythos. Er ist der rennsportliche Archetyp des Ur-Elfers. Grund genug für viele Fans, sich an eine Rekonstruktion des spartanischen Racers zu wagen. Und geradezu ideal, wenn man bereits ein Original besitzt, an dem alle Maßnahmen abgeglichen werden können. Es folgt: die Jungfernfahrt, Kopf-an-Kopf-Vergleich von Original und auf ST umgerüstetem S-Modell. Teil eins: Rennstrecke. Teil zwei: Bergstrecke.

Die alte Formel-1-Rennstrecke im österreichischen Spielberg ist ideal für diesen Trainingslauf geeignet. Schnelle Bögen, lange Geraden, harte Winkel – das dürfte Herausforderung genug sein. Mit Dampf durch die schnelle Rechts am Ende der Start/Ziel-Geraden: Die Stabilität stimmt. Dann wieder alles an Leistung aus den Motoren holen, es geht bergauf, dann hart auf die Bremse, Rechtsknick. Alles ist da: Die Sechszylinder marschieren mit Macht, die Bremsen dominieren nachdrücklich, die Balance sitzt. Im folgenden Links-Links-Rechts-Feuerwerk müssen die 911 ST schon nichts mehr beweisen, hier legen sie sich nur noch die finale Mutkurve zur Start-Ziel-Geraden zurecht.

Und drei Runden später steht der Entschluss fest: Übermorgen treffen wir uns im ersten Sonnenlicht am Stelvio. Ob die hochgezüchteten Rennmotoren auch mit dem unsteten Drehzahlwechsel, den Schwebesekunden am Berg klarkommen, mit der dünnen Luft und den untertourigen Momenten, das will nämlich ebenfalls getestet werden. Zumindest ist das die wunderbar seriös klingende Ausrede. In Wahrheit können wir es kaum erwarten, das flammende Duo auf unserer Lieblings-Serpentinenstrecke auszuführen. Rennstrecke und Passstraße, das sind einfach zwei Welten. Wir lieben den Präzisions-Infight in den geometrisch ausgelegten Radien einer gut gemachten Strecke. Aber die Tour zum Stilfser Joch ist eine Herzensangelegenheit. Hier sind wir Könige.

At the start of the 1970s, Porsche's racing department built a true rarity. Designed for endurance racing and rallying, the scarcity and racing success of the 911 ST secured its place in motoring folklore. It's the racing archetype of the Ur-911. Reason enough for many fans to venture a reconstruction of the spartan racer. And it's especially fortuitous when you already own an original to serve as a benchmark. So here we have it – the maiden outing, head-to-head comparison of an original and an S-Model converted to an ST. Part one – racetrack. Part two – mountain road.

The old Formula One racetrack in the Austrian town of Spielberg is ideally suited for this training session. Fast arcs, long straights, hard angles – it should be challenging enough. Foot down through the fast right-hander at the end of the first straight. The stability is just right. Take all the power the engine has to give for the uphill stretch, then go hard on the brakes for a kink to the right. It's all there – the six-cylinders marching forcefully, the brakes dominating emphatically, the balance perfect. In the left-left-right explosion that follows, the 911 STs don't have anything left to prove, all that's left to despatch is the final test of courage before the home straight.

And three laps later the decision has been taken – we'll meet the day after tomorrow at the Stelvio at sunrise. We also want to test whether the thoroughbred engines are able to deal with the erratic rev changes, the airborne seconds on the mountain, with the thin air and the low-speed torque. At least, that's the wonderfully serious sounding excuse. The truth is, we can hardly wait to take our flaming duo out on our favourite serpentine. Racetrack and mountain pass – simply worlds apart. We love the precision infighting in the geometrically arranged radii of a well-built track. But a trip to the Stelvio Pass goes much deeper. This is where we reign supreme.

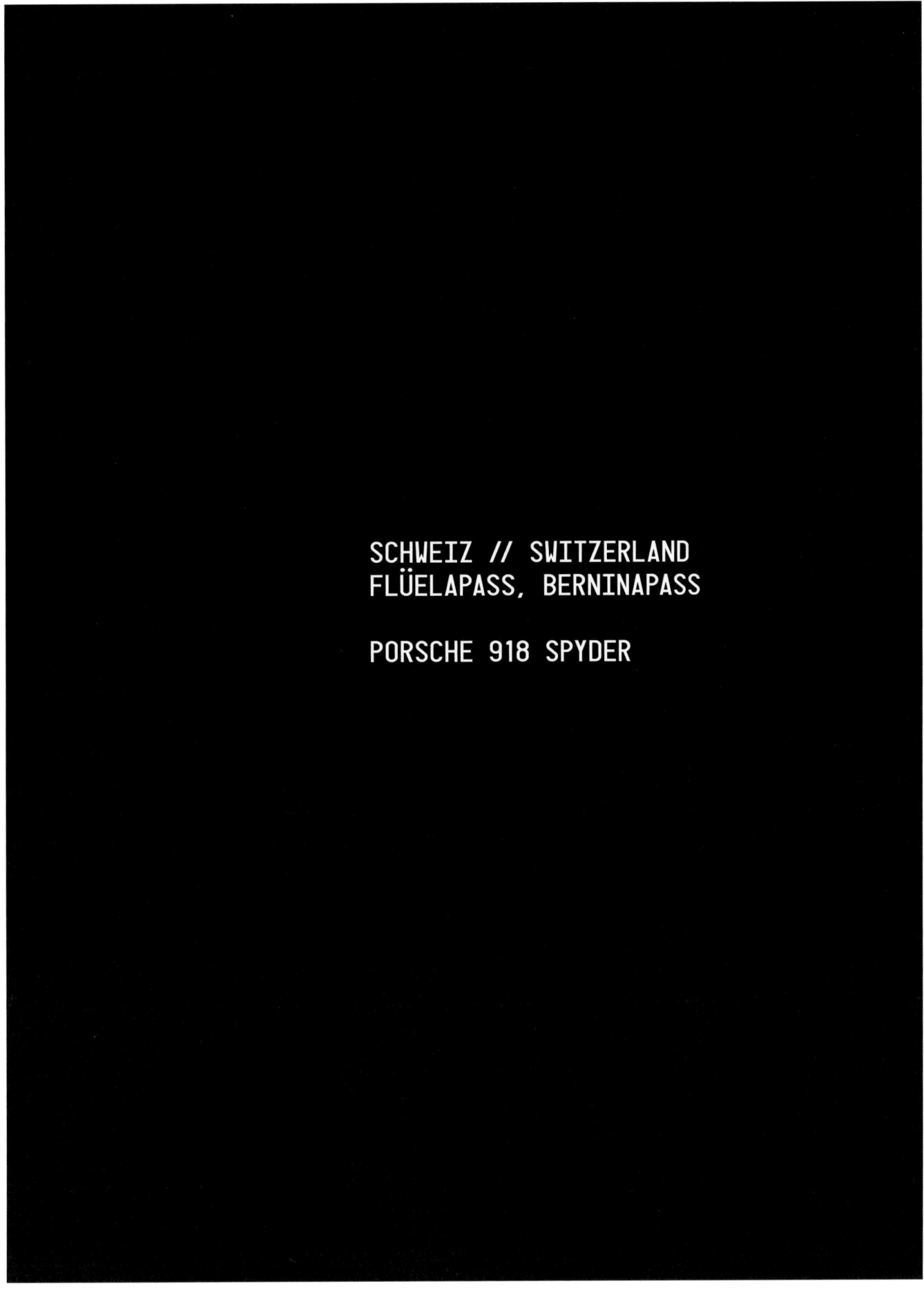

PORSCHE 918 SPYDER

Kälteschlaf ist keine Option. Der ganzjährig offene Berninapass und die in Segmenten vom Schnee befreite Straße zum Flüela ziehen magisch an. Gut, dass wir Winterreifen für unseren Porsche 918 Spyder gefunden haben.

Hibernation is not an option. The Bernina Pass, which is open all year round, and those sections of road to the Flüela cleared of snow, look magical. It's a good thing that we managed to find winter tyres for our Porsche 918 Spyder.

Hinter uns der Süden Italiens. Hochgeschwindigkeitsrunden mit dem Porsche 918 Spyder auf der Teststrecke in Nardo. Und jetzt muss das Auto irgendwie nach Hause kommen. Der Platz im Transporter ist bereits reserviert. Aber wir schütteln den Kopf: Raus aus Apulien, über die Abruzzen vorbei an Rom, Umbrien rechts liegen lassen, quer durch die Toskana, Emilia-Romagna, die Lombardei – und dann über die Berge. Erst in diesem Moment entdecken wir den Fehler im Detail. Es ist Winter. Außer den großen Tal- und Tunnelrouten, den Wintersport-Zubringerschneisen haben die Alpen jetzt geschlossen. Die Pässe träumen unter meterhohen Schneedecken vom Sommer. Einen Moment lang scheint der Traum vom langen Weg nach Hause so flüchtig wie Pulverschnee. Nicht mit uns. Jetzt erst recht. Und außerdem gibt es ja den Berninapass. Der geht beinahe immer.

Die Technik-Crew der Teststrecke mag zuerst nicht so recht, aber dann findet sich doch noch ein passender Satz Winterreifen für den 918. Am Abend sehen wir die weißen Gipfel der Alpen in der Sonne glänzen, am nächsten Morgen wachen wir umgeben von Bergen auf. Die Strecke über den Berninapass, von Bianzone bis Sankt Moritz, ist vor ein paar Tagen präpariert worden. Nahezu schneefrei zieht sich das Asphaltband den Berg hinauf, lediglich ein paar eisige Stellen packen etwas Spannung in die Querung. Kein Problem für den 918 Spyder. Der hat dank E-Motor an der Vorderachse eine ganz besonders pfiffige Form von Allradantrieb, zieht eiskalt seine Bahn, und als wir im Engadin angekommen sind, herrscht große Enttäuschung: Soll das Winterabenteuer bereits zu Ende sein? – Nicht ganz: Hinter Zernez wechselt der Flüela rüber nach Davos, die Strecke ist zwar nicht in ihrer Gänze zu machen, hat aber auch im Winter viele Kilometer weit offen, wenn das Wetter passt. Und heute passt es. Wintersonne satt, kristallblauer Himmel, milde Temperaturen ziehen dem Spyder das Dach herunter. Sahnige Drifts mit 887 PS Systemleistung, Bergluft im Cockpit, genau so haben wir uns das vorgestellt.

Southern Italy lies behind us. High-speed laps on the Nardo test track with the Porsche 918 Spyder. And now, we have to get the car home somehow. There's already a space reserved for it in the back of the van, but we shake our heads. Out of Apulia, past Rome via Abruzzo, then Umbria on the right, all the way through Tuscany, Emilia-Romagna, Lombardy – and then over the mountains. It's at this point that we spot the problem with our plan – it's winter. Aside from the major valley and tunnel routes – the main arteries for winter sports traffic – the Alps are now closed. Buried under metre-thick blankets of snow, the passes dream silently of summer. For a moment, the dream of the long road home seems as fleeting as powder snow. But not for us – definitely not now. And besides, there's always the Bernina Pass. It's almost always clear.

The technical crew at the test track don't like the idea at first, but then manage to find a set of winter tyres to fit the 918. That evening, we see the white Alpine peaks glistening in the sun and the next morning we awake surrounded by mountains. The road over the Bernina Pass from Bianzone to St. Moritz was prepared a few days previously. Almost completely free from snow, the strip of asphalt snakes its way up the mountain. Only one or two icy patches give the crossing a modicum of thrill. The 918 Spyder takes it in its stride. Thanks to its electric motor at the front, it has an especially smart form of all-wheel drive and sticks steadfastly to its line the whole way through. There's a pervading sense of disappointment by the time we reach Engadin – is the winter adventure already over? Not quite: beyond Zernez, we take the Flüela over to Davos. Although we're not able to drive the road in its entirety, many miles of it are open even in winter if the weather is onside. Which it is today. Bright winter sun, crystal-blue skies and mild temperatures pull the Spyder's top down. Creamy-smooth drifts with a system output of 887 hp, mountain air in the cockpit – exactly as we had imagined it.

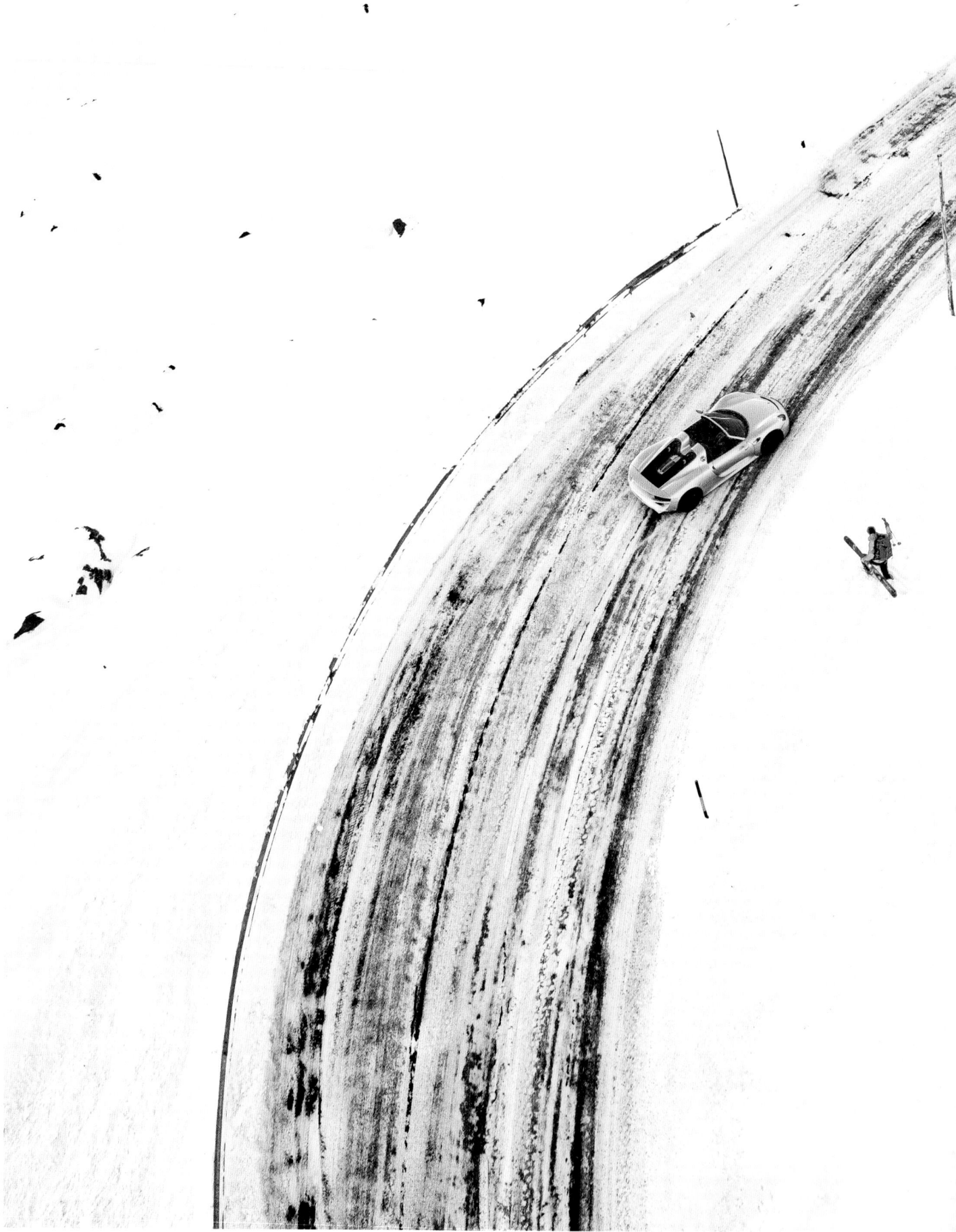

DEUTSCHLAND // GERMANY
WEISSACH

PORSCHE 911 GT2 RS
PORSCHE MISSION E

PORSCHE 911 GT2 RS
PORSCHE MISSION E

Ein Treffen der Extreme. Porsche Mission E und 911 GT2 RS auf dem Testgelände in Weissach. Außenstehende dürften diesen surrealen Moment eigentlich nicht erleben. Aber heute ist für wenige Minuten alles anders.

A meeting of extremes. The Porsche Mission E and 911 GT2 RS on the Weissach proving grounds. Outsiders weren't really supposed to experience this surreal moment. But today, for just a few minutes, everything is different.

Weissach im Herbst. Die Porsche Teststrecke liegt versteckt in den Hügeln, aus den Äckern ringsum weht ein milder Wind den mürben Duft von Erde heran. Obstbäume stehen in den Wiesen, das Laub zeigt eine erste rostrote Färbung. Ein Tag mit entspanntem Ruhepuls – wenn da nicht die beiden Porsche wären, die sich auf eine der großen Asphaltflächen im Infield des Testgeländes pirschen. Strahlend weiß in der linken Ecke der Mission E, feuerrot und schwarz in der rechten Ecke der 911 GT2 RS. Der rein elektrisch angetriebene Sportwagen der Zukunft und das brachiale Rennstrecken-Werkzeug der Jetztzeit sind verschiedene Charaktere – und trotzdem schöpfen sie aus einem gemeinsamen Gen-Pool. Kompromisslose Performance und maximale Effizienz, radikale Fahrdynamik durch den Einsatz von an die Grenze des Machbaren getriebener Technologie. Die beiden Porsche sind an diesem Tag im Herbst 2017 beinahe noch Phantome: Dem GT2 RS steht seine Serienfertigung erst bevor, der Mission E hatte noch nicht einmal Premiere. Ab 2019 wird das Serienfahrzeug debütieren, der kurz zum Fototermin erschienene Prototyp ist dann bereits ein Fall für die Ahnengalerie.

Heute aber fühlen sich die beiden flüchtigen Geister keineswegs wie eine Erscheinung an. Sondern vollkommen real. Mit kernigem Motorsound stürmt der GT2 RS auf die Strecke, der Mission E folgt dicht dahinter. Völlig geräuschlos, regelrecht schattenhaft, und trotzdem sehen die Beobachter: Der ist schnell. Sagenhaft schnell. Ohne Geräuschkulisse haben die Sinne ein Problem, den Anblick des davonzoomenden weißen Elektro-Sportwagens mit der gehörten Realität übereinanderzuschieben, und das macht alles nur noch dramatischer. Auf der Strecke gehört das Hier und Jetzt dem 911 GT2 RS, er fährt wie im Traum, präzise und Physik-verbiegend. Ein Fahrgefühl wie die Zeitlupe-Actionszenen in Science-Fiction-Filmen. Wenn das nicht perfekt zu diesem Moment zwischen Gegenwart und Zukunft passt.

Weissach in autumn. The Porsche proving grounds are hidden away in the hills, surrounded by fields, the mellow fragrance of earth drifting in the mild wind. The meadows are dotted with fruit trees, their leaves just starting to turn rust red. All-in-all, it would be a very relaxed day – if it weren't for the two Porsches prowling around on one of the big patches of asphalt in the proving ground's infield. Gleaming white in the left corner, the Mission E; fire red and black in the right corner, the 911 GT2 RS. The all-electric sports car of the future and the brutal racetrack machine of the present day are different characters – yet products of the same gene pool. Uncompromising performance and maximum efficiency, radical dynamics delivered by technology pushed to the very limits of feasibility. On this day in autumn 2017, these two Porsche are still more or less phantoms – the GT2 RS is almost ready for production, while the Mission E hasn't even been premiered. The first production vehicle will debut in 2019, by which time the prototype that appeared briefly for the photo shoot will already have taken its place in the ancestral gallery.

Today, however, the two fleeting spirits seem like anything but apparitions. They feel very real indeed. The GT2 RS storms onto the track with a throaty roar; the Mission E following behind, completely silently, a veritable shadow. Yet those watching can see very clearly – it's fast, phenomenally fast. Without the usual soundtrack, the senses are faced with the problem of overlaying the sight of the zooming, white electric sports car with the aural reality, making the experience all the more dramatic. On the track, the here-and-now belongs very much to the 911 GT2. It drives like a dream, precise and in defiance of the laws of physics. It feels like the slow-motion action scenes from a science-fiction movie. What a perfect fit for this moment between present and future.

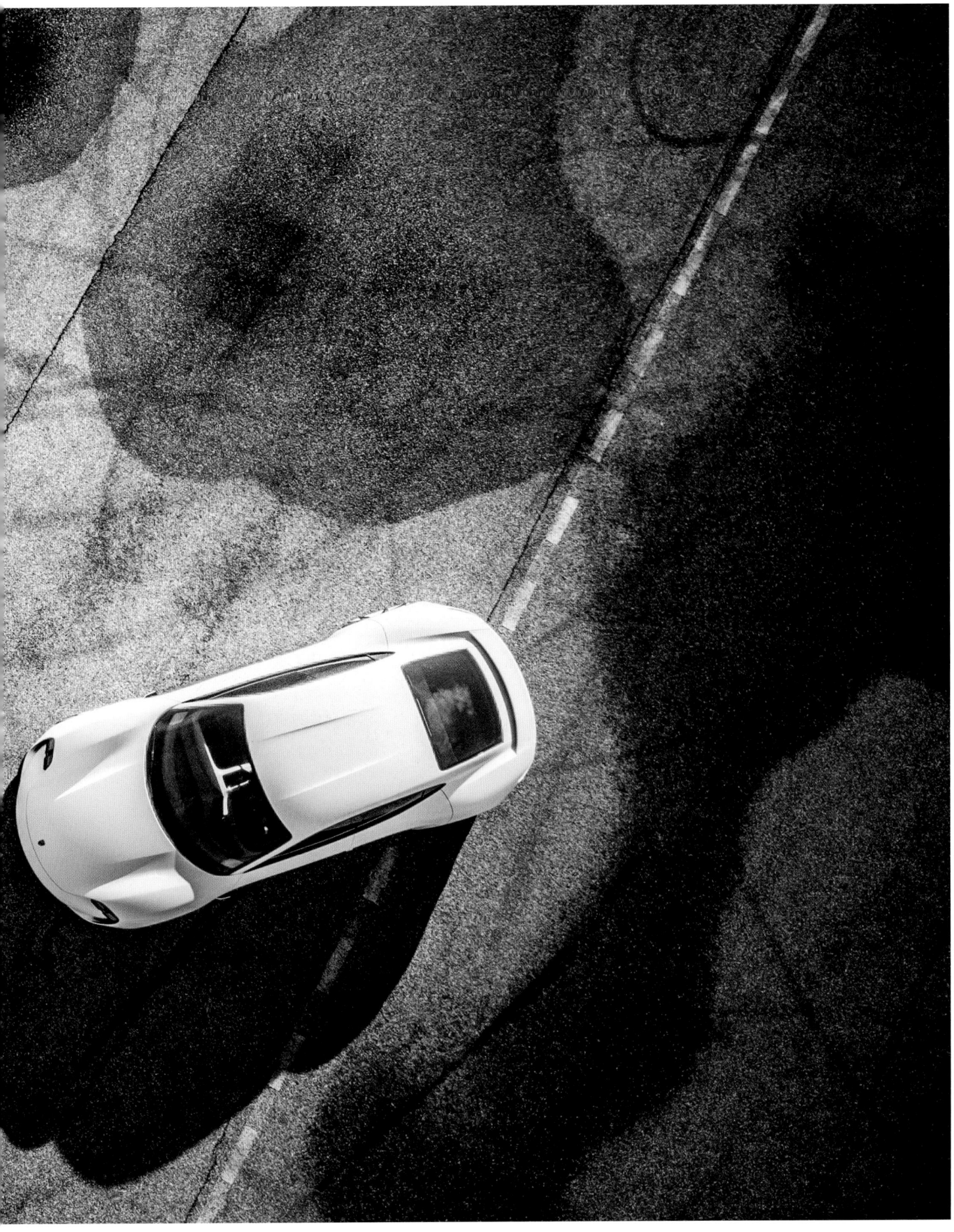

ITALIEN // ITALY
SIZILIEN // SICILY
TARGA FLORIO

PORSCHE 718 CAYMAN

PORSCHE 718 CAYMAN

Da oben in den Hügeln wartet die Herausforderung. Das Magnetfeld der Erde wird von diesen 72 Kilometern regelrecht gebeugt, ein Gravitationsfeld für Racer entsteht. Targa-Florio-Land.

The challenge lies up there in the hills. The Earth's magnetic field is well and truly bent by these 72 kilometres. The result is a gravitational field for racers. Targa-Florio land.

Auf Sizilien ist irgendwie immer Targa Florio, im Porsche sowieso. Anbremsen von Kurven unter uralten Olivenbäumen, ein scheinbar schwerelos von Schatten zu Schatten hastender Porsche 718 Cayman auf Zeitreise. Entfesseltes Einlenken in die nächste Kurve, während dahinter ein Berg seine Eingeweide in samtblauen Himmel spuckt, die Felstürme des Gebirges sich vor eine glühende Sonne schieben oder ein sattgrünes Tal hoch oben an den Wolken in einem plötzlichen Windstoß fröstelt.

Unten auf der SS 113 am Meer hatte man früher sieben Kilometer Zeit zum Durchatmen, um die verkrampften Finger vom Lenkrad zu brechen oder auch nur um mal wieder zu blinzeln. Ausatmen, einatmen, die Nackenmuskeln einmal durchrollen, dann sind auch schon die knackigen Bögen entlang einer Natursteinmauer hoch zur Start-Ziel-Geraden da. Und heute die bleichen Beton-Gerippe der alten Boxen-Anlage. Dicht gefolgt von den ersten, berückend intensiven Kilometern in die Berge hinein. Dann: Cerda. Die Targa hat aus der Durchgangsstraße steil den Berg hinauf eine Rennstreckengerade gemacht, die schnellsten Rennwagen der 1960er fallen über den Ort als eine Explosion aus kreischendem Sound zwischen den Hauswänden mit 300 km/h her. Erinnerungs-Gänsehaut im Cayman, diese Rückblende ist kaum vorstellbar. Immer weiter saugt uns die Runde in die Madonien-Berge.

Kurze Geraden heucheln Entspannung, sind aber so wellig und zerfurcht, dass man sie beinahe mit noch größerer Konzentration einwickeln muss als die Kurven. Die Straße besitzt jedoch eine herrliche Musikalität, sie öffnet und schließt sich, pulsiert ganz hart und atmet dann wieder ganz weich. Schroffe Felszinnen ragen aus den Hügeln, sagenhaftes Panorama. Vor Caltavuturo links weg in Richtung Scillato, Collesano ist nach den kühlen Höhenlagen feucht und warm, das Auto schnürt durch die engen Gassen und nimmt dann die letzten Kilometer hinunter nach Campofelice. Zurück am Meer. Unser Porsche 718 Cayman rollt vor Hitze knisternd aus. Die Targa Florio ist vorbei. Oder doch nicht?

Somehow, it's always Targa Florio on Sicily – and even more so with a Porsche. Braking into corners beneath ancient olive trees – a Porsche 718 Cayman seems to flit between the shadows on a journey through time. Turning freely into the next bend, while a mountain in the background disgorges its innards into the velvet-blue sky, the towering rocks push their way in front of a glowing sun or a lush green valley high up in the clouds shivers in a sudden gust of wind.

In the good old days, when you were down at the coast on the SS 113, you had seven kilometres when you could breathe a little easier, loosen your cramped fingers from around the steering wheel or even just blink. Breathe out, breathe in, roll out your neck muscles, the you're into the tight bends along a stone wall leading up to the home straight. And today, the bleached concrete carcass of the old pits, followed closely by the first irresistibly intense kilometres into the mountains. Then comes Cerda. The Targa turned the steep uphill thoroughfare into a racing straight. The fastest race cars of the 1960s descended upon the town at 300 km/h in an explosion of screaming sound bouncing off the buildings. Sitting in the Cayman, the memory causes goose bumps. This flashback is almost incomprehensible. The lap pulls us farther and farther into the Madonie Mountains.

Short straights seem to offer respite, but are so bumpy and potholed you almost have to afford them even more concentration than the bends. Nevertheless, the road possesses a glorious musicality. It opens and closes, pulsates hard then breathes softly. Rugged rock battlements rise majestically from the hills – it's a stunning panorama. Just before Caltavuturo you take a left towards Scillato. After the cool altitude, Collesano is humid and warm. The car purrs through the narrow streets before embarking on the final kilometres down to Campofelice and back to the sea. Our Porsche 718 Cayman coasts gently to a halt, sizzling hot and popping. The Targa Florio is over. Or is it?

ÖSTERREICH // AUSTRIA
RED BULL RING

PORSCHE 904 CARRERA GTS

PORSCHE 904 CARRERA GTS

Die Welt des Rennsports ist klein, eine verschworene Gemeinschaft Gleichgesinnter. Da kann es schon passieren, dass dein Auto einer Legende gehört hat. Porsche 904 Carrera GTS, Vorbesitzer: Sir Stirling Moss.

The racing world is small – a close-knit community of likeminded people. It's always possible that your car once belonged to a legend. Porsche 904 Carrera GTS. Previous owner: Sir Stirling Moss.

Klassische Rennwagen sind Zeitmaschinen. Sie erfordern keinen musealen Intellekt und keine Interpretation, um mit ihnen in die Vergangenheit zu reisen, sie funktionieren ohne Umwege und regelrecht intravenös. Ihr Sound, ihre Kraft und ihr Charakter übertragen sich direkt auf den Fahrer, der auf der Stelle mitten im Erleben ist: Genau so war das früher. Kein Historiker kann besser erzählen.

Auch mit dem Porsche 904 Carrera GTS von 1964 liegen die Dinge nicht anders. Seine Karosserie aus glasfaserverstärktem Polyesterharz und der pragmatische Stahlkastenrahmen erzählen die Geschichte vom niederschwelligen Einstieg in den Kundenrennsport, nach dem sich die Porsche Fans Mitte der 1960er-Jahre verzehrten. Mindestens 100 Exemplare mussten reglementskonform für die GT-Klasse gefertigt werden – kein Fall für eine aufwendige Konstruktion mit Stahlrohrrahmen und gedengelter Leichtmetallkarosserie. Kurze Notiz ans Unterbewusstsein: Schon damals war Porsche ganz vorne, was den Einsatz innovativer Technologien anbelangt: Rennsport ist ein ultimativer Antrieb. Dann geht es über die hohen Schweller hinein ins Cockpit, der Vierzylinder-Boxermotor dominiert jetzt alles. Laut, martialisch und energisch erobert der Carrera GTS die Rennstrecke, er fährt herrlich exakt und hellwach.

Knapp 55 Jahre alt und kein bisschen angegraut, die alte Rennmaschine hat gefühlt kaum Patina zugelegt. Nach einigen Eingewöhnungsrunden ertappt man sich bereits bei den üblichen Spätbrems-Kampflinie-Spielchen, die man dem alten Kämpen eigentlich nicht zumuten wollte. Aber hier stimmen einfach die Reflexe, Racer bleibt Racer. Vor dem inneren Auge zeichnet sich ein naturgetreues Abbild der Sechziger, als dieser Carrera GTS ein modernes, pfeilschnelles Gerät war. Dass wir diesen Moment mit Sir Stirling Moss teilen, für dessen Rennstall unser 904 einmal an den Start ging, ist dann beinahe keine Überraschung mehr. In der Welt klassischer Automobile überschneiden sich die Linien oft überraschend, im Rennsport wird alles noch intensiver.

Classic race cars are time machines. They demand neither museum intellect not interpretation to travel into the past. They do so with no detours and completely intravenously. Their sound, their power and their character transfer directly to the driver, who is transported immediately into the thick of the action. Just as it was in times gone by. There isn't a historian around that can tell it better.

And it's no different for the 1964 Porsche 904 Carrera GTS. Its bodyshell made from glass-fibre-reinforced polyester resin and the pragmatic steel box frame tell the tale of low-level entry into customer racing, longed for by Porsche fans in the mid-1960s. At least 100 of them had to be built to conform with GT-class regulations – not a case for a sophisticated design with a tubular steel frame and hand-beaten aluminium body panels. Brief note to the subconscious – even back then, Porsche was at the forefront when it came to the use of innovative technologies. Racing is the ultimate motivator. You climb over the high sills into the cockpit, the four-cylinder boxer motor dominates everything – the Carrera GTS is loud, menacing and energetic in its domination of the race track, running with magnificent precision and fully alert.

Almost 55 years old and not a grey hair on its head, the old racing machine feels like it's gained barely an ounce of patina. After a few laps to settle in, you can already feel yourself subjecting the old war horse to the usual aggressive, late-braking games that you actually didn't expect of it. But the reflexes are simply there. Once a racer, always a racer. In your mind's eye, you sketch out a lifelike image of the sixties, when this Carrera GTS was a modern, lightning-swift piece of machinery. The fact that we're sharing this moment with Sir Stirling Moss, in whose racing stable our 904 once competed, is somehow almost no longer a surprise. In the world of classic automobiles, the lines are often astonishingly blurred. In racing, everything becomes more intense.

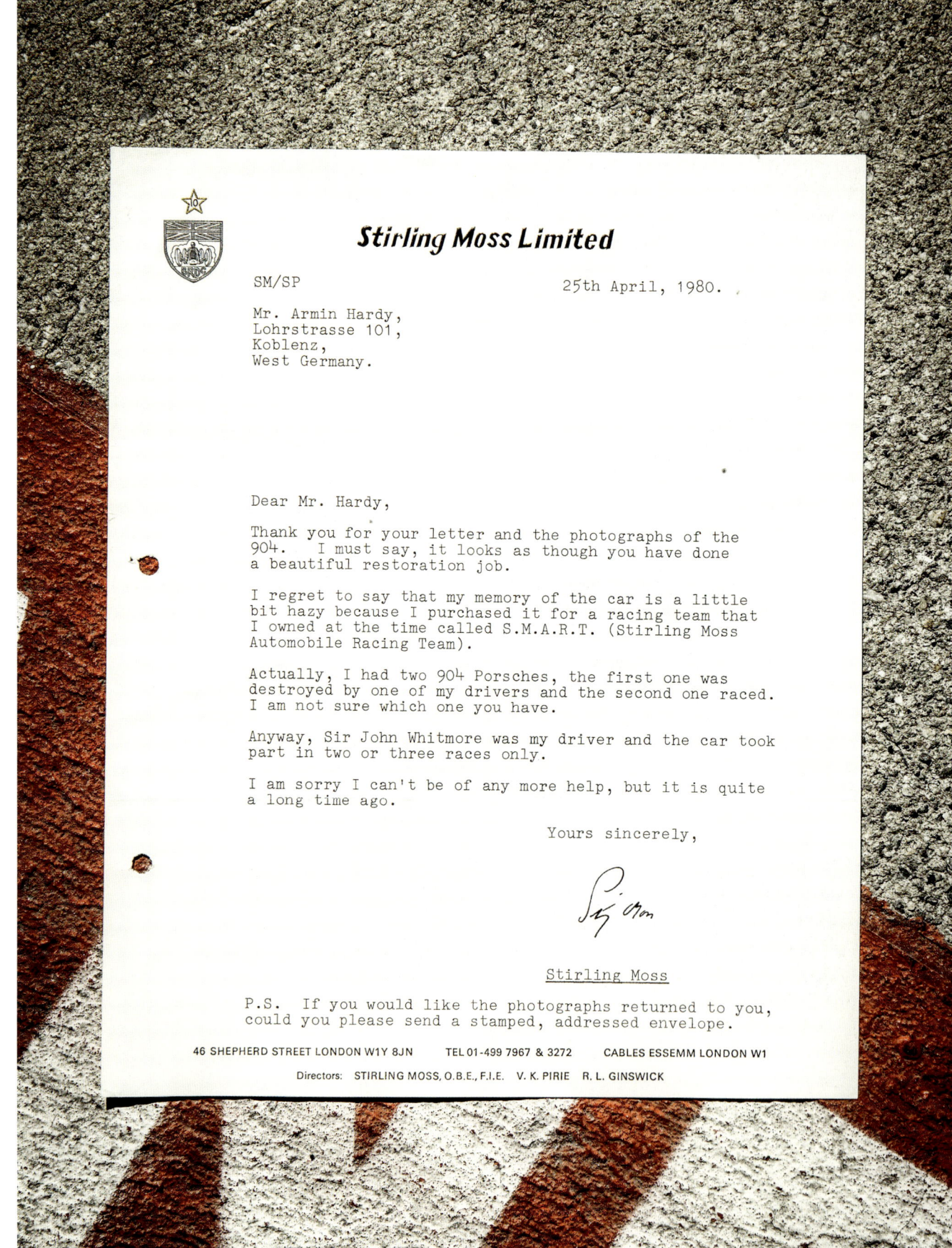

ÖSTERREICH // AUSTRIA
ITALIEN // ITALY
GROSSGLOCKNER – DOLOMITEN

PORSCHE 911
PORSCHE 911 ST RECREATION
PORSCHE 964 RS
PORSCHE 964
PORSCHE 911 GTS

PORSCHE 911
PORSCHE 911 ST RECREATION
PORSCHE 964 RS
PORSCHE 964
PORSCHE 911 GTS

Davon träumen wir einen ganzen, langen Winter lang: die erste Fahrt einer Saison über die Alpen. Die besten Porsche 911 aus sieben Jahrzehnten. Nomaden-Freunde beim Gipfeltreffen. Besser geht nicht.

It's what we dream of all winter long – that first drive of the season over the Alps. The best Porsche 911s from seven decades. A summit for nomadic friends – it can't get any better than this.

Der Plan wird bereits vor Weihnachten geschmiedet, erste Routenvorschläge fliegen per E-Mail hin und her. Route des Grandes Alpes und Seealpen bis ans Mittelmeer? – Die Riesenpässe der Zentralschweiz? – Runter nach Venedig? – Zumindest so viel steht fest: Graues Winterwetter ist ein hervorragender Katalysator, um sich in die Ferne zu wünschen. Im Januar und Februar haben die Sehnsuchts-Routen immer etwas mit Sonne und Meer zu tun, klar. Das ist wie hungrig einkaufen gehen, du bleibst automatisch vor den dicksten Würsten und dem Schokoladenregal stehen. Eines wissen aber alle: Wer zu viel will, bekommt ganz schnell überhaupt nichts.

Die epischen Fahrten in den Süden werden deshalb verschoben, die Eckdaten für den Saison-Start sind schließlich überschaubar: Freitagmittag aus dem Büro, Samstag Königsetappe, Sonntagabend zu Hause. Mehr geht nicht. Und mehr muss auch nicht sein. Hauptsache: Raus! In unserem Fall dreht sich die Zirkelnadel auf der Landkarte in München, mehr als 250 Kilometer Luftlinie Radius schaffen wir nicht – und auf einmal ist alles klar: Die Großglockner-Hochalpenstraße ist perfekt zum Einschwingen, im Drau-Tal geht es direkt an die Grenze nach Italien. Dann die Dolomiten-Runde bis Bozen und zurück über den Brenner. Ab jetzt heißt die Grundstimmung: Hochgefühl statt Winterblues. In den Garagen wartet ein Rudel der besten Porsche 911 aller Zeiten, da sind wir in unserer Einschätzung ganz unbescheiden und subjektiv. Der elfenbeinweiße Ur-Elfer vertritt die edlen Anfänge, mit einer Recreation des legendären 911 ST zünden wir klassische Schnell-und-Leicht-Dramatik, der 964 RS namens „Sternrubinchen" ist immer wieder für augenöffnende Kurvenkombinationen gut und im modifizierten 964 vollkommen unorthodoxer Machart wird der Traum vom Porsche unerschrocken hemdsärmelig. Bis die Helden aber laufen dürfen, sitzen wir in Garagen am Steuer und träumen. Dann wird es Mai. Die Verkehrsmeldungen verkünden: „Alle Pässe offen!" – Jetzt beginnt der Sommer, jetzt beginnt das Leben.

The plan was already forged before Christmas with the first route suggestions flying to-and-from via email. The Route des Grandes Alpes and the Maritime Alps to the Mediterranean? – The grand passes of central Switzerland? – Down to Venice? – At least one thing is certain, grey winter weather is an excellent catalyst for wanderlust. In January and February, these tantalising routes always have this association with sun and sea – obviously. It's a bit like going grocery shopping when you're hungry – you automatically stop at the juiciest sausages and in the confectionary aisle. But we all know for sure that if you want too much, you very quickly end up with nothing at all. The epic drives south are thus postponed and the cornerstones for the start of the season end up far more manageable – we leave the office Friday lunchtime, do the main stage on Saturday and head home on Sunday. We can't do more than that – and we don't have to either. The main point is to get out! In our case, the circle on the map centres on Munich. We can't manage more than a radius of 250 kilometres as the crow flies. And suddenly it all becomes clear – the Grossglockner High Alpine Road will do perfectly, then through the Drau Valley all the way to the border with Italy. We follow that with a lap of the Dolomites as far as Bolzano and back across the Brenner. The winter blues immediately switch to an almighty summer high.

Waiting in the garages is a pack of the best Porsches of all time – with no room for modesty or objectivity in our assessment. The ivory white Ur-911 represents the noble beginnings, with fast and lightweight drama provided courtesy of a recreation of the legendary 911 ST. The 964 RS known as "Ruby Starlet" is always good for eye-opening curve combinations, and in the totally unorthodox and modified 964, the Porsche dream becomes unashamedly laid-back. However, until these heroes are allowed to run, we sit at the wheel in garages and dream. Then May comes around. The traffic news announces: "All passes open!" – summer starts now; life starts now.

Wir danken allen, die uns in den letzten Jahren begleitet und unterstützt haben. Ob daheim oder on the road – ohne euch wären die Magazine und Bücher der letzten Jahre und dieses Buch nie entstanden. Danke an alle Fans auf Skateboards, Bikes, Motorrädern und in Autos, die die gleiche Leidenschaft teilen.

We express our thanks to all those people who have accompanied and supported us in the past few years, either at home or on the road. Without you, this work and all the other books and magazines of the last years wouldn't exist. Thanks to all enthusiasts on skateboards, bicycles, motorbikes and in cars who share the same passion.